MISSION Mania

A Can-Do Guide for Youth
Leader's Guide

Mission Mania
A Can-Do Guide for Youth

Scripture quotations in this publication, unless otherwise indicated, are from the New Revised Standard Version of the Bible, copyright ©1989 by the Division of Christian Education of the National Council of the Churches of Christ in the United States of America, and are used by permission. All rights reserved.

The writers and editors of *Mission Mania* would like to thank the following persons for appearing on the cover and within the pages of this publication and the student component, *Mission Mania: Crazy to Serve:* Casey Barnaby, Patti Barnaby, Ashton Brown, Leah Bushor, Cathy Elmore, Katy Elmore, Kyle Elmore, Robyn Elmore, Kaci Hickox, Ginny King, and Giovanna Saylors.

Ty B. Powers, *Editor*
Kevin Happell, *Production Editor*
Keely J.P. Moore, *Design Manager*
David Arnold, *Designer*
Susan Scruggs, *Designer*

 **Abingdon Press**

00 01 02 03 04 05 06 07 08 09—10 9 8 7 6 5 4 3 2 1

Vital Verses

"The greatest among you will be your servant. All who exalt themselves will be humbled, and all who humble themselves will be exalted."

(Matthew 23:11-12)

Contents

What Is *Mission Mania?*

▲ *Mission Mania* is more than a one-time weekend service project during which youth volunteer for community service.

▲ *Mission Mania* is more than service-learning, because the fact is that experiential learning can often occur with little or no reflection on God's presence and transforming power. *Mission Mania* intends to re-commission that omission!

▲ *Mission Mania* happens when persons discover, develop, and utilize their God-given passion and gifts within the context of Christian service.

▲ *Mission Mania* occurs when Christians, while striving to transform a lost and hurting world for Christ, are transformed themselves by the God whom they serve.

▲ *Mission Mania* is a life-transforming, life-energizing, faith-developing process!

▲ *Mission Mania* changes people! Once persons have been consumed with the joy that *Mission Mania* brings, they'll never be the same—they'll go back again and again to serve others for Christ!

How Do I Use *Mission Mania?*

Mission Mania can be used with junior high and senior high youth either separately or together. It's also appropriate for college-age students and intergenerational groups.

Mission Mania is flexible enough for any number of settings:
▲ As an essential part of a traditional five-session Vacation Bible School program, with the option for a subsequent service-oriented follow-up
▲ As part of an evening fellowship
▲ As a single weekend retreat, either separate from, or in conjunction with, a week-long VBS program
▲ As a special-occasion mission opportunity
▲ As a one-time *Mission Mania* week at church
▲ As various mission opportunities that become available
▲ As a "pre-VBS" *Mission Mania* experience for those congregations with youth on the VBS staff
▲ As an introductory event to a service opportunity at the end of VBS

Get Inside This Leader's Guide!

Mission Mania: A Can-Do Guide for Youth is full of great stuff that will help you turn your youth group into an enthusiastic crowd of "Mission Maniacs." The introductory section (pages 4-14) provides practical information for getting a service project up and running smoothly. The main body of this guide (pages 15-55) is divided into three main sections or "tracks"—*In Class, On the Go,* and *Weekend/Retreat*—each devoted to a distinct service approach depending on the particular needs of your group. Finally, the list of *100+ Double M Service Ideas* (pages 56-63) offers creative ways your group can reach out to persons in need. Whatever your style, *Mission Mania* will work for you and your youth.

Track #1 — In Class (pages 15–47)

▲ Use this approach for a traditional daytime or evening Vacation Bible School. Do one session per day.

▲ If you want to lead a five-week study on the topic of service, use one session per week. This is ideal for any weekly youth setting. Consider culminating the study with an off-site, hands-on mission project.

▲ If you'd prefer to extend the study beyond five weeks, customize the five sessions to your needs. Each session contains various activities that can be used to extend the study beyond five weeks.

▲ If you want material for less than five sessions, simply pick and choose from the existing material. The five sessions can be used sequentially or can stand alone as special one-time lessons on service.

▲ If you want to study *Mission Mania* in a five-week, hour-long Sunday school setting, customize sessions by omitting discussion questions, shortening activities, and so forth.

Each in-class session follows a specific format:

▲ *Your Goals* helps you know what to expect from your group by the end of the session.

▲ *The Stuff You Need* is a list of supplies, including those items for optional activities.

▲ *Start Up* includes opening activities connected to the session's theme. These help set the mood and encourage the participants to get to know each other.

▲ *Mission Mania in the Bible* presents Scriptures and activities that should impress upon the participant that service and love for others have always been God-given mandates.

▲ *Their Turn* is the central part of each session. Students can put the session's theme into action through a significant activity. Each activity should include a Debriefing section during which the youth reflect and discuss what they have just experienced. **Never forget to debrief!**

▲ *Plan a Mission Possible!* suggests optional hands-on service ideas for the group to plan. Use this time with the group to perform later in the week or month.

▲ *The Closing* offers meaningful ways to end the session and prepare the participants' hearts for the next session.

Each element of the pattern contributes to the life-transforming potential of *Mission Mania*. It is recommended that you lead the sessions in this order*:

1. **Choose at least one *Start-Up* activity.**
2. **Do *Mission Mania in the Bible* in its entirety.**
3. **Choose at least one *Their Turn* activity. *Never forget to debrief!***
4. **Do the *Closing*.**

*   **Special Note:** *Plan a Mission Possible!* is optional and therefore not included in the recommended pattern. You will need to designate specific time for it if you decide to include it. Here are a few options for using your class time well:

   • Plan out the Mission Possible and be ready to go before the youth come to *Mission Mania*. One drawback to this option is that it doesn't involve the youth in the decision-making process. It's important that the entire group gain a sense of ownership in any group activity.

   • Select one or two youth to research available Mission Possible opportunities in your community and ask them to present their findings during the time when the whole group gets together.

   • Use the Mission Possible time to involve the entire group in the decision. Youth will get a chance to interact with you and with each other.

Track #2 — On the Go (pages 48-50)

▲ Use this approach if you and your youth prefer off-site, hands-on mission experiences.

▲ This approach is effective if your youth are part of a VBS volunteer staff, yet are not formally gathering during the daily VBS festivities.

The On-the-Go approach is flexible for any mission project because it allows you to choose which service event best suits your group's needs. Choose from the list of Double M Service Ideas that begins on page 56 or come up with your own event. The suggested Scriptures and guidelines for discussion and debriefing will work with any event. All you need to do is apply your group's specific constraints to the general guidelines, and you're on your way to a successful service project!

Track #3 — Weekend/Retreat (pages 51-55)

▲ Use this approach if you and your youth prefer an overnight or weekend hands-on mission experience.

▲ This approach can stand alone or be paired with the two other approaches in various combinations. For example, plan a one-time special mission event, or culminate a five-day VBS In-Class *Mission Mania* experience with a weekend out-of-town service retreat. ***The possibilities are endless!***

The Weekend/Retreat approach works best when several mission events are experienced over the course of the retreat. Larger groups will need to divide into smaller service teams that either work at different tasks in the same facility or that travel to different projects within the same city. On pages 52-55, you'll find both suggestions for helping you have a successful weekend service retreat and a sample schedule.

Ten Tips for Connecting With a Mission Mania Agency

One of the first things you need to do is consider which agency will fit your group's goals and collective personality. Use these tips, along with the list of more than 100 Double M Service Ideas, which begins on page 56.

▲ Ask anyone who has had first-hand contact with local caregiving agencies or ministries: a friend, a fellow youth pastor, your pastor, or your church's mission committee. Ask how they got started.

▲ Look in the Yellow Pages under "Social Service Organizations" or "Churches."

▲ Call your local chamber of commerce or city hall.

▲ Call your local chapter of the United Way, American Red Cross, Meals on Wheels, Salvation Army or other similar organization.

▲ Call the denominational offices of your church. Ask about committees or groups devoted to social services, volunteer organizations, or mission opportunities.

▲ Consult your local police department or fire department. They often know of care-giving agencies or ministries in your area.

▲ Search the Internet. Go to a search engine and type in such topics as "mission," "service," "youth ministry," or "volunteers." Also search your denomination's websites.

▲ Consult social workers at your local hospital or other care-giving facilities. Don't overlook child protective services, job placement, family services, night shelters, and other groups specializing in community social work.

▲ Drive around your community. Look carefully for possible mission projects. We often overlook opportunities because we are not looking with the compassionate eyes of Christ.

▲ If you already know of agencies in your community, call them. If they don't need your assistance, they may be able to refer you to other local agencies needing help.

Three Essential Steps for Any Mission Project

Step 1: Briefing

Providing a sufficient amount of pre-trip information is crucial.

Before the Project:

▲ Choose a different project for each session. More than 100 Double M Service Ideas are listed starting on page 56. Or think up a project on your own.

▲ Choose a project that you and everyone else can get excited about!

▲ Call, visit, and make scheduling arrangement with the work site.

▲ Choose and get permission to use a debriefing site. Do this in advance.

▲ Give youth and parents plenty of information about the project and work site.

▲ Address adequately any questions or concerns.

▲ Let youth and parents know accurate departure and return times.

▲ Inform youth and parents about relevant policies, restrictions, forms, and fees.

▲ Inform youth and parents about equipment needed.

▲ Let parents know where the work site is and how to contact you during the trip.

▲ Depending on the work site, chaperones may need to serve as supervisors.

▲ If there is an overabundance of available tasks for everyone, encourage the chaperones to be active participants. Otherwise, encourage them to serve as "positive observers/helpers."

The Day of the Project:

▲ Always begin and end the event with prayer. Ask for God's blessings throughout the day's activities.

▲ Make sure that the youth understand that they should never make fun of others. While they assuredly can have a good time, their behavior should reflect respect and compassion.

▲ Make it clear that youth should never wander off alone. Establish a place to meet in case someone gets lost.

▲ Encourage the youth to interact with new people, striking up conversations and listening carefully to the stories being told.

▲ Tell the youth to "dig in"! It should be one of the few activities when they are actually encouraged to get their hands dirty.

▲ Encourage everyone to do their best to be polite, positive, respectful, and flexible. Things don't always go as planned.

Step 2: Connecting

Sharing God's love can be a wonderful, life-transforming experience for youth.

▲ This is the portion of the trip where everyone gets to get their hands dirty.

▲ Always read the day's Bible passage, preferably from a contemporary translation. See page 49 for the list of On-the-Go Suggested Daily Scriptures.

▲ Ask the teenagers to be participants, not mere spectators.

▲ The chaperones should take the last available work stations. Give the teenagers the first choice.

▲ Remind the youth to be polite, respectful, helpful, and positive at all times. They should treat all others as children of God.

Step 3: Debriefing

Reflecting on the day's experiences is perhaps the most essential ingredient of any successful **Mission Mania** *project. This can be a time when long-lasting personal growth occurs.*

If you've never included debriefing in your group meetings, now is a good time to start. For detailed debriefing guidelines, see pages 9-10.

▲ *Debriefing is definitely one step NOT to rush.* Life transformation is not a thing to be hurried!

▲ Ask the questions (also known as The Five *T's*) from the Daily Debriefing section (page 10). They're a great way to get the conversation flowing. Remind the participants that their student component, *Mission Mania: Crazy to Serve,* provides room for writing down answers to the questions you're asking. (If you're running short on time, you may need to select specific questions from the list. Just don't eliminate this process altogether. Debriefing can be a very meaningful time for everyone.)

▲ Debrief as soon as possible following the project, preferably the same day and on-site (with permission, of course). If circumstances don't allow, schedule a debriefing session as soon as possible, while the event is still fresh on the minds of the participants. *Whatever the case, don't eliminate the debriefing altogether. It's essential!*

▲ Remember that reflection can be an effective time during which the day's experiences converge with a teenager's Christian faith. Debriefing gives youth the opportunity to reflect on how the experience was a faith-shaping and life-changing event.

▲ Encourage (but don't force) the youth to talk openly about their experiences, both positive and negative. Be equally supportive of the participants who may have had a negative experience.

▲ Ask everyone to take this process seriously. It may be a time when God touches people's lives, teaches them something new, or inspires them to do something new.

▲ Remind the adults not to dominate the debriefing process. Though it's helpful for the chaperones to discuss their thoughts and reflections, encourage the teenagers to do most of the talking.

▲ Don't forget to choose and get permission to use a debriefing site *in advance.*

▲ Find a place where you won't be easily distracted or disturbed.

▲ If possible, debrief outdoors or in another special setting.

▲ Always conclude with prayer.

Daily Debriefing

Debriefing is a necessity, especially when it comes to something as experiential as mission trips and service projects. It gives the youth a chance to talk about the day's experience and to contemplate how God is using them to reach others.

Why Bother With It?

Debriefing is essential because:

▲ It gives teenagers an opportunity to talk about their experiences.

▲ It allows them to address their own feelings.

▲ It gives them an opportunity to express their joys, frustrations, fears, likes, and dislikes.

▲ It challenges them to reflect on the day's experiences.

▲ It provides a forum where they can ask and grapple with tough questions.

▲ It gives you an opportunity to clarify intentions, address problems, and to affirm their service.

▲ If gives them an opportunity to hear other students' experiences and reflections, and to see how mission work has affected others.

▲ It helps them see how their faith and experiences are related.

▲ It provides a setting in which important issues can be addressed (for example: homelessness, AIDS, poverty, hunger, prejudice, stereotypes).

▲ It helps to create meaningful memories.

▲ It helps to develop a sense of unity.

▲ It helps to connect them with God.

And for those who prefer educational theory:

▲ It moves students from the concrete to the abstract.

▲ It moves students from simple recall to higher levels of the cognitive domain.

▲ It helps to integrate theology with life experience.

▲ It is based on the educational process known as service-learning.

A Debriefing Guide for Any Mission Event

Another reason why debriefing is so essential is that the reflection it prompts has the potential to transform an ordinary service project into an extraordinary faith-developing event.

Debriefing involves five important steps, called The Five T's (page 10). The teenagers begin by talking about their concrete experiences and conclude by reflecting on the transforming qualities of the experience. For consistency's sake, each time you hold a mission event, debrief using the same Five *T's*. The accompanying student piece to this guide, *Mission Mania: Crazy to Serve,* follows the five-step method given here and provides room for reflection or journaling for up to five mission events. When the time comes for debriefing, make sure you have a copy of the Five *T's* on the next page to prompt you through the debriefing process.

Give your youth an opportunity to respond to these questions. ***Never make anyone feel uncomfortable for not responding.*** Some teenagers may simply want to watch, listen, and think. Others won't mind sharing their thoughts and feelings. Without allowing any one person to dominate the debriefing, ask for volunteers (teenagers and chaperones) to respond. If you are running short on time, it may be necessary to select specific questions from this list. Just don't eliminate this process altogether. ***Debriefing is crucial!***

Finally, make sure the adults don't dominate the debriefing process. Though it's great for the adult chaperones to share their thoughts and reflections, encourage the teenagers to do most of the talking. Debriefing gives the youth an opportunity to reflect on how this experience was a faith-shaping and life-changing event.

The Five T's

Step 1: Tell

This step asks, "What did you experience?" Encourage teenagers to talk about their concrete experiences—what they saw, touched, smelled, heard, did. Save reflection for another section. This is simply the recollection of what they experienced.

1. What did you see and experience today?

2. Describe the work site, the task you performed, and the people with whom you worked.

Step 2: Touch

This step asks, "How did this experience make you feel?" Did it make the youth feel happy, important, useful, sad, frustrated, afraid, warm inside, indifferent, angry or what? If they are willing or able, have them explain their responses.

3. Explain why you did or did not enjoy your task. Explain why it did or did not make you feel uncomfortable. Explain why you would or would not mind doing this kind of work again. If you were able to go back, what, if anything, would you do?

4. How did others respond to your help?

5. How do you suppose it made them feel? How did it make you feel?

Step 3: Teach

This step asks, "What did this experience teach you about God? About others? About yourself?"

6. How did today's Bible passage relate to what we did today? (See page 49 for recommended Bible passages.)

7. What, if anything, did your experience have to do with your Christian faith? How is the act of serving others also an act of serving God?

8. Because of this experience, what are some of the things you learn about God? About other people? About yourself?

Step 4: Transform

This step asks, "How did this experience transform your attitudes, concerns, stereotypes, lifestyle?"

9. How has today's project changed your attitudes in any way (for example, about poverty, homelessness, the elderly, and so forth)?

10. Because of today, what will you notice now that you've never noticed before?

11. What can we do as a youth group to make a further impact in this area? When should we begin?

Step 5: Take It to Heart

This step asks, "What do you want to take away from this experience?"

12. What's one thing you want to remember about today's experience?

13. What made today's experience memorable?

Remember to have the youth take their student guide, *Mission Mania: Crazy to Serve*, to the mission site. They may get inspired. The daily journaling section of the student guide follows this exact five-step process.

Good Teams Make the Mission!

Don't try to do everything yourself. Enlist teenagers and adults to help with your service project. *Teams should consist of teenagers and adults who have an interest in a particular type of work.* However, if you find that you have, for example, 25 people who love to hammer and one person who likes to saw, then you will need to divide teams up so no one gets overworked. Of course, the number of teams will vary from project to project. Here are some suggested "positions" you will want to consider filling.

Each of these teams would be accountable to the project coordinator—that is, either you or someone to whom you have assigned this responsibility.

The **Project Coordinator** plans, oversees, and implements the project. He or she should make sure the church carries liability insurance for off-site injuries and that the drivers are covered under the church's automobile insurance. The Project Coordinator typically leads debriefing sessions. This person could very well be you!

The **Publicity Team** is responsible for putting up posters, writing newsletter articles, making public announcements, and anything else that will let your congregation and community know what your Mission Mania event is all about.

The **Spiritual Enrichment Team** leads lessons and devotions (and possibly the debriefing sessions). Don't overlook the possibility of having older teens as members or leaders on this team. With enough support and pre-trip training, reliable teens can do a wonderful job with this.

The **Registration Team** is the group of persons responsible for "signing up" participants and making sure they have paid any necessary fees for such items as lodging, meals, and other incidentals. Consider setting up a registration table or getting team members to enlist participants by making appeals in youth Sunday school or other weekly youth group meetings.

The **Food Preparation Team** ensures that there are enough drinks, food, and snacks for everyone. Some groups prefer to bring their own food while others prefer to eat out.

The **Transportation Team** is responsible for having enough drivers and vehicles for the event. Consult your church's administrative offices for possible age restrictions established by the church insurance policy.

The **Set-up/Cleanup Team** sets up, brings cleaning supplies (like brooms, buckets, and trash bags), and does an excellent job of encouraging everyone to help with clean up. A good motto for this team is, "Leave the place looking better than it did when we started."

The **Equipment Team** gathers and brings any necessary supplies or equipment (like rakes, paint brushes, work gloves, and so forth).

The **Service Teams** are responsible for the actual work. This includes everyone (unless he or she is hindered by a medical or handicapping condition). When determining these teams, don't segregate by gender or age; instead form groups based on shared interest. Teenagers and adults should work side by side. Unless instructed otherwise, you should bring at least one adult per seven teenagers; and teams should not exceed 6-8 members.

20 Questions to Ask Your Prospective Mission Organization

Here are some general questions you can ask prospective mission organizations. Depending upon the nature and length of your project, some may not be necessary.

> **Note:** *If possible, take a pre-trip to your* Mission Mania *work site. It will be easier to make decisions about a facility you've seen firsthand. See page 54 for more details.*

1. Do you accept junior high students as volunteers? Senior high students? Girls and boys? Entire youth groups? Are chaperones allowed to bring their younger children? Will you be able to accommodate any youth with special needs or disabilities?

2. Do you have any restrictions on the number of participants who come?

3. Do you require special Medical Release or Liability Release forms to be signed or notarized?

4. Do you expect a certain number or ratio of adult chaperones to attend?

5. Do you offer, recommend, or require pre-service training?

6. Do you have any clothing restrictions, for example, no shorts, no sandals, no caps, no bandannas?

7. Will the teenagers need to bring any special equipment (like tools, goggles, hard hats, work gloves, hair nets, rubber gloves, aprons, flashlights) or clothing (like stuff that can get wet or paint-splattered; or of a certain weight or fabric, such as jackets)?

8. Exactly what type of work will the teenagers be doing? Typing, filing, sorting, stocking, cleaning, lifting, tutoring, recreation, childcare, VBS, or what? Indoors or outdoors? Will the teenagers be sitting, standing, walking? Will all of the teenagers work together? In small groups? Individually? Supervised or unsupervised? Will they be working in the same building or location? Will there be plenty of work to do?

9. When and how long will we be needed? Are the days and times flexible? Do we need to register our group in advance or do you allow "drop-ins"?

10. Will there be any on-the-job supervision and training? If so, how many adults have you scheduled to work with our teenagers? What security, if any, will you provide?

11. Do you have plenty of bathrooms (accessible to people with disabilities), water fountains, pay phones, ice, drink machines, snack machines, and first-aid supplies? If not, are there any stores or snack shops nearby? Do you have a change machine?

12. Will you provide any snacks, drinks or meals? If not, are there any places to buy food nearby?

13. Are there any items my youth should not bring? (Some places don't allow portable radios, CD players, cameras, or video recorders. Others don't allow such things as pocket knives or bottled drinks.)

14. Are there any customs, policies, or procedures that I need to be aware of? If we will be working with an ethnic group, what can you tell me about this group's unique needs?

15. Who is the contact person? Is there a particular day and time he or she can be reached? Can this person be reached by email, cell phone or beeper? Will I be notified if the event has been canceled or postponed?

16. In the event of an emergency, how can parents contact their teenagers at the facility?

17. What are the goals of this particular project (and this agency in general)? Ask for promotional brochures, business cards, and their Web site information.

18. Is it hard for you to get volunteers? (Ask them to explain their answer.)

If You're Staying Overnight

19. Do the teenagers need to bring sleeping bags, cots or air mattresses, pillows, towels, oscillating fans (some places don't have air conditioning in the summer), or portable heaters (some places are cold in the winter)?

20. Do you have shower facilities? Are the bathrooms dorm style or "suite" style? How are the sleeping facilities arranged and where are they located? Are they well-lit? Do you have a security guard? Do we need to bring any lamps, air freshener, bug spray, ice chests, toilet paper, trash bags or anything else? Will we have access to cooking facilities?

Through the Eyes of Jesus

**TRACK #1
(In-Class Sessions
Begin Here)**

Your Goals

Teenagers will . . .
◆ See what it's like to "view the world through the eyes of Jesus."
◆ Look into the world of persons who are homeless and become more sensitive to their plight.

We recommend leading the session in this order:
1. **Choose at least one *Start-Up* activity.**
2. **Do *Mission Mania in the Bible* in its entirety.**
3. **Choose at least one *Your Turn* activity. Never forget to debrief. (See page 9 for why debriefing is so important.)**
4. **Do the *Closing*.**

The Stuff You Need

◆ Bibles
◆ Poster board or large sheets of paper
◆ Plenty of copies of closing prayer (page 21), printed on colored paper

SUPPLIES FOR OPTIONAL ACTIVITIES

For *Photo Fun Start Up* activity (page 16)
◆ Duplicate prints of 15-20 photographs showing several normal objects at very close range, with only a portion of the item photographed.
◆ Several felt-tip markers

For *Building a Cardboard Community* activity (pages 18-19)
◆ Plenty of large cardboard boxes. *Hint:* Furniture stores and businesses that sell appliances like refrigerators and air conditioners are great places to get large cardboard boxes. If you tell them what you're doing and give sufficient notice, many of them will save boxes for you! Some grocery stores are willing to save small and medium boxes too.
◆ Rolls of duct tape and twine
◆ A few sharp knives or box cutters
◆ A flashlight
◆ Two or three pillows and two or three old blankets
◆ Wheelchair, pair of crutches, and one or two walking canes (or walkers)
◆ Garden hose, water sprinkler, or large fan

Start Up

Being observant is the key to winning!

More than mere icebreakers, these activities emphasize this session's theme—seeing the world through the eyes of Jesus. Explain that being observant is the key to winning—both in the context of playing games and, more importantly, in serving others. Say something like: "If we as Christians try diligently to observe our environment, we'll become increasingly aware of opportunities to serve others."

NOTES

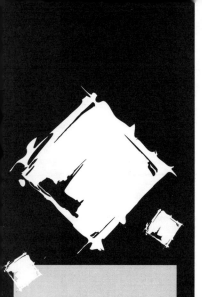

Wink

Divide the group in half, with one more person being in Group A than in Group B. If you have an equal number of youth, one counselor will need to join one of the groups. Have the members of Group A take one chair each and put in a circle facing inward. (If you have more than fifty youth, make two circles.) Members of Group A stand behind their chairs with their hands behind their backs. Group B members sit in the chairs, except for one chair that is left vacant. The person behind the vacant chair (the Winker) must get one of the Group B members into that chair by winking at them. The person who has been winked at (the Winkee) tries to get out of the chair without being tagged by the person behind her or him. If tagged, the person must remain in the chair, and the Winker tries again, by winking at another person. If the Winkee can get out of the chair without being tagged, she or he takes the chair in front of the Winker, and the person with the vacant chair is now the Winker. Anyone who can avoid becoming the Winker is the winner. Halfway through the game, have the two groups switch places.

Photo Fun

Supplies Needed: Have someone take 15-20 photographs of several everyday objects at very close range, photographing only a portion of the item. Have duplicate prints made. Provide a felt-tip marker for each team.

Divide into two teams and give each team a complete set of the photos. Have them try to figure out what is in each picture and write their answers on the back. When the youth have identified as many objects as they can, have them present their guesses. The team with the most correct answers wins.

Mission Mania in the Bible

Jesus and Persons in Need: A Radical Perspective

Mark 10:13-16

Read or have one of the youth read aloud the Scripture once, then proceed to "What's So Radical?" and discuss the questions.

What's So Radical?

Ask:
1. Why were Jesus' actions in Mark 10:13-16 considered radical?
2. How do you think the treatment of children in Jesus' time was different from the way people treat children today?
3. Who in our society is treated the way children were during Jesus' time?
4. How is Jesus' treatment of the children different from the way people treat persons who are homeless in today's society? How is it similar?
5. If Jesus were here today, how would he treat persons who are homeless? Explain.
6. In your opinion, what does it mean to "see the world through Jesus' eyes"?

In Jesus' day, children, persons with disabilities, and those who were poor were generally treated as non-persons—persons who had nothing to contribute to society. When Jesus said, "Let the little children come to me; do not stop them," he was being radical! He did not address the children using derogatory terms; instead he embraced them and blessed them! Jesus included everyone; no one was left out.
When Jesus looks at people, he sees their needs. As Christians, we can do the same thing when we look at people whom society considers worthless. Encourage the youth to "see the world through Jesus' eyes." They'll have a radically new perspective.

NOTES

Take Another Look at Scripture

Have someone reread Mark 10:13-16. However, this time, have them substitute the word homeless (or homeless person) for the word little child or little children.

> People were bringing the homeless to him in order that he might touch them; and the disciples spoke sternly to them. But when Jesus saw this, he was indignant and said to them, "Let the homeless come to me; do not stop them; for it is to such as these that the kingdom of God belongs. Truly I tell you, whoever does not receive the kingdom of God as a homeless person will never enter it." And he took them up in his arms, laid his hands on them, and blessed them.

Your youth need to understand that people become homeless for a variety of reasons. There's a story behind every person's misfortune. Tell the youth to pretend that they are visiting a night shelter, where they meet the following persons who are homeless. Beforehand, write the following descriptions on poster board or newsprint and tape them up around the room. Instruct the youth to read each one, paying particular attention to how each one became homeless.

At the age of 16, **Sarah** was pregnant. She and her boyfriend Jason got married. Since they couldn't afford to live on their own, they remained at Sarah's house until their baby was a few months old. Explaining that the financial and emotional burdens were just too much to bear, Sarah's parents forced Sarah, Jason, and the baby out of the house. Jason's old car is their only shelter.

The **Taylors'** rental home was destroyed by a tornado. All five of them are now living at a night shelter. Mr. Taylor also lost his at-home business. They don't have the money to rebuild.

Jim, a mentally ill patient discharged from a psychiatric hospital, is an embarrassment and hardship to his family. They don't have the patience, energy, or finances to help him.

Fifty-year-old **Mr. Butler** has worked in the same factory most of his life. With the arrival of new technology and state-of-the-art machinery, his skills are no longer needed—anywhere. He finds himself unable to afford his house payment and car payment. He feels like he has no choice but to head for the streets.

Bob is unemployed. With an eighth-grade education and limited job training, he doesn't have the education or skills to get a job that pays a living wage.

Kenneth has struggled with alcohol and drug abuse for years. His situation became so serious that he was evicted from his house. With no immediate family in the city, he hit the streets.

With no family, only limited support from government, and no financial aid for a nursing home, 75-year-old **Mrs. Smith** has no place to live.

Kate ran away from an abusive situation at home.

Discussion
1. What are some of the words that perhaps you have used or you have heard people use when referring to persons who are homeless? (Examples: *bum, tramp, hobo, an embarrassment to the community, a blight on society, freeloader, panhandler, beggar, delinquent, slacker, loafer, drifter*)
2. Why do you think some people have such negative opinions about persons who are homeless?
3. How does labeling someone sometimes stop us from ministering to his or her needs?
4. Which of these persons would you most likely help? Why?
5. Which of these persons would you least likely help? Why?
6. How would you help him or her? Why? For how long?
7. Which of these would least likely find help in today's society? Which would easily find help? Why? How does that make you feel?
8. What issues must you address when answering these questions? (Examples: prejudice, misinformation, stereotypes)
9. Which of these persons would Jesus help? Explain.

Their Turn

You'll find two options for letting youth have their turn. Both activities are designed to help your students "see the world through the eyes of Christ." Through what they learn in today's session, some of your teenagers actually will "see" the issue of homelessness for the first time or in a whole new light. Choose the option that is best suited for your group. Always debrief—it's essential!

Building a Cardboard Community

A great way to heighten teenagers' awareness of the plight of persons who are homeless is to have them construct a cardboard community somewhere on your church property or another suitable location. This activity will help youth realize how limited the resources are for a person who is homeless. Remind the youth that during his ministry, Jesus daily encountered individuals much like the characters they're about to portray. Encourage them to really get into their roles, to make them as authentic as possible.

Objective
Everyone in the cardboard community needs to have a dry place to sleep within the time limit (90-120 minutes). This is not a race to see who can get finished first or who has the best-looking structure. The goal is to construct a sturdy shelter using relatively few resources.

Cardboard Community Guidelines
1. Divide the youth into family groups. Each family is responsible for building its own cardboard house, which should be big enough for the entire family to fit. If your youth group is small enough, make the youth all members of the same family. Family groupings might look like the following, but feel free to create other "family units" at your own discretion. Be creative!

    A pregnant mother with two small children
    A family of five with an aging grandparent
    A mentally-challenged man or woman with his or her friend
    Two or three runaway teens
    A family that just became homeless because the sole breadwinner's employer went bankrupt.
    An adult man and women, with his brother and sister-in-law and their children
    A war veteran in a wheelchair and his two teenagers

2. Try not to give the youth any ideas on how to build their homes. They need to work through the difficulties of planning and building the structure themselves.

3. The structure should be durable enough for people to move around in it. It also should keep out the elements, particularly the wind and the rain! For added obstacles (if you're outdoors), make your own weather for the cardboard community with a hose or a sprinkler. Use a big fan to create a wind storm. Remember that it can get a little messy, so make sure you get permission before setting up.

4. It should have some sort of flooring, so the youth are not sleeping on the ground.

5. If it is necessary to get permission to conduct this type of project, get it in advance.

6. Each person should function according to his or her assigned role. Children wouldn't be able to lift as much as most of the adults and so forth.

7. Bring fewer supplies than you would actually need. That way, the groups will be forced to share the knives, twine, and duct tape in order to meet the goal.

8. Always use care when handling the knives.

9. So that everyone has a sense of pride and dignity, each participant must have an active part in building a home, regardless of situation. No one is simply to be a spectator.

10. Once everyone has a cardboard home in which to sleep, ask the entire group to decide who should get the flashlight, the pillows, and the blankets. Again, let the teenagers be the decision-makers, basing their rationale for distributing these items on the character descriptions provided at the beginning.

Some groups might want to make this an overnight event—sleeping in the cardboard houses and debriefing in the morning.

Debriefing

Find a comfortable place to sit near the cardboard homes and discuss the following questions. Give your teenagers an opportunity to respond to these questions. As always, don't force anyone to respond. Some teenagers may simply want to watch, listen, and think. Others won't mind sharing their thoughts and feelings. Without allowing any one person to dominate the debriefing, ask for volunteers (teenagers and chaperones) to respond to the following.

1. What did you see and experience today?

2. Would you describe the work site? The task you performed? The people with whom you worked?

3. What's one thing you want to remember about today's experience? Why?

4. What did you enjoy about your task? Why? What made you feel uncomfortable? Why? If you did this activity again, how would you do it differently?

5. How did others respond to your help?

6. How do you suppose it made them feel? How did it make you feel?

7. How did today's Bible passage relate to what we did today? Explain.

8. How did your experience connect with your Christian faith?

9. Because of this experience, what are some of the things you learned about God? about others? about yourself?

10. How has today's project changed your attitudes in any way (for example, about poverty, homelessness, the elderly, your stereotypes, and so forth)?

11. How did you decide who would get the flashlight, the pillows and blankets? Were your decisions based on stereotypes or actual needs? How did it make you feel to be responsible for deciding who should and who shouldn't get these "extras"?

12. Because of today, what will you notice now that you've never noticed before?

13. What can we do as a youth group to make a difference in our community? When should we begin?

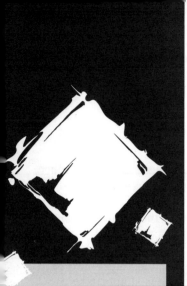

A Guest Speaker: The Plight of Persons Who Are Homeless

Have a social worker, night shelter manager, clergy, or someone who works with persons who are homeless talk to your teenagers. This person could either be paid or volunteer staff. If he or she has traveled a great distance or works professionally with persons who are homeless, consider providing an honorarium. Ask him or her to talk about the following:

◆ What it's like to live on the streets
◆ The type of person who lives on the street
◆ How people end up living on the streets
◆ The difficulties in getting off the streets once a person becomes homeless
◆ What agencies, churches, and other ministries are doing to help
◆ What his or her particular group does to help (some may have a promo video to show)
◆ How your group can help

Conclude with Questions and Answers. To avoid putting your youth on the spot, preview with them who the speaker is and his or her topic and ask them to formulate their own questions beforehand.

Plan a Mission Possible!

1. Take the teenagers on a prayer tour of the impoverished area(s) of your town (or a nearby town). As you drive by, look for signs of poverty, homelessness, people without jobs, signs of hunger, hurt, and despair. At safe places on the tour, stop your vehicle and pray for needs that that you or the youth observe. Ask God to bless those in need and think of practical ways your group can bless them.
2. Go on a blanket run or sack lunch run. Take blankets or sandwiches to persons who are homeless under bridges, sleeping in cars or boxes, or living on the street. If it's cold, you might want to take hot soup or coffee. Take plenty of adults as chaperones.
3. Visit a night shelter. See firsthand what it's like to be a person who is homeless. This provides an excellent opportunity for the youth to interact with the shelter's visitors, to find out about people's background, families, aspirations, and so forth. Remind the youth that they aren't required to talk about homelessness. It simply may be an excellent time to forge a new friendship. Just remember: encourage—don't pressure—your youth to interact.

Closing

Provide everyone with copies (on colored paper, if you like) of the following prayer with the commitment section covered. In unison, read the prayer out loud. At the end of the entire Mission Mania experience, return with copies of this same prayer (this time with the commitment section included) printed out on heavy card stock or decorative certificate-style paper. Invite those who are ready to sign and make a commitment.

A Prayer for Serving Others

I believe in God, Creator of the world;
and in Jesus Christ, the Redeemer of creation.
I believe in the Holy Spirit,
through whom I acknowledge God's gifts.
I commit myself to the rights
and dignity of all persons
and to the improvement of the quality of life.
I dedicate myself to peace
throughout the world
and to the rule of justice
and law among all nations.
I believe in the present and final triumph
of God's Word in human affairs,
and gladly accept my commission
to manifest the life of the gospel to the world.

_____

I hereby make this commitment today!

_____   _____
Signature   Date

NOTES

LOVE 2

for others

Your Goals

Teenagers will . . .
- Discover what "love for others" really means
- Learn that love can motivate them to take action to make a difference!

We recommend leading the session in this order:
1. **Choose at least one *Start-Up* activity.**
2. **Do *Mission Mania in the Bible* in its entirety.**
3. **Choose at least one *Your Turn* activity. Never forget to debrief.**
4. **Do the *Closing*.**

The Stuff You Need

- Bibles

For *Mission Mania in the Bible* (page 23)
- Assorted props for *The Great Debate* activity. (See page 23 for more details.)
- Chalkboard and chalk, large pad of paper or markerboard and markers

SUPPLIES FOR OPTIONAL ACTIVITIES

For *Things I Love* activity (page 23)
- Index cards

For *"Too-Young Yolanda" Comic Strip* activity (page 25)
- Large sheets of paper and lots of colored markers

Start Up

What's love got to do with it?

Use at least one of these icebreakers to help youth focus on God's type of love and remember this session's theme—that God gave us the responsibility to share God's love with others, often through the gift of service. As you continue, emphasize that people sometimes label certain emotions as love when they actually mean something else, and that when it comes to serving others, actions often do speak louder than words. To enrich the discussion of the different meanings of the word "love," find a good Bible dictionary and research briefly and be prepared to present various Hebrew and Greek words for love including *hesed* (steadfast love), *agape*, *philos*, and *eros*.

NOTES

Darling, If You Love Me, Smile!

Ask the group to sit in a circle. The object of this game is to make the other person smile or laugh. Choose someone to be "it." This person must now choose another player in the circle as his or her "victim." Whoever is "it" kneels in front of the victim and says, "Darling, if you love me, smile." The victim must reply, "Darling, I love you, but I just can't smile," without smiling or laughing. If the victim does smile, then he or she is "it." If he or she doesn't smile, whoever is "it" must choose another victim. Whoever is "it" can do anything possible (make faces, gesture wildly, talk with an accent, twirl hair) to make the other person smile. *A few rules: 1) no tickling; 2) no touching the victim's face; and 3) victims must look whoever is "it" directly in the eyes at all times.* Give the game a time limit, and make sure everyone gets at least one chance to be a victim.

Things I Love

As the youth arrive, have each one make a list of five things he or she loves on an index card. Invite them to write their names on the back of the card. Place the cards in a container, mix up the cards, and choose cards one by one, read the clues one at a time, and have people guess who it is.

Mission Mania in the Bible

Samuel and Eli: Can Teenagers Really Make a Difference?

1 Samuel 3:1-20

Read or have one of the youth read the Scripture aloud once, and then proceed immediately to the "The O.T. Files—Voices in the Night" activity.

The O.T. Files—Voices in the Night

Divide the class into groups of three. Invite them to present a 2-3 minute dramatic paraphrase of 1 Samuel 3:1-20. Modernize the scene by setting it around an mysterious campfire in a scary forest, on a road trip to the grandparents' house, or in the middle of a one-on-one basketball game. Or come up with your own setting. Have the other youth add appropriate sound effects.

Take Another Look at Scripture

Reread 1 Samuel 3:1-20 aloud. Then tell the group that it's time for a Great Debate.

The Great Debate

Set this activity up like a wacky quiz show, with the "pro" side on one side and the "con" side on the other. Get a volunteer to keep time. Choose one of the following options before you get started. (Options 2, 3, and 4 will take some planning ahead of time.)

1. Divide the group into two teams. Ask one team to speak against the argument and the other to speak for it. If the group is large, use different teams for each question.
2. Invite several respected (and articulate) members of your church to serve as a debate panel. Ask them to take one side of the argument while the teenagers take the other side. If your group is large, have a new team step up for each question.
3. Invite parents of teenagers to debate the youth.
4. To provide a forum for interaction with other teenagers, invite several teenagers from another church to take one side of the argument while your group takes the other side.

Have each group choose a spokesperson. Begin the debate by announcing, "Today's debate: Can teenagers really make a difference in the world?" Use a flip chart, chalkboard, or markerboard to introduce each question. Treat the debate like a speed round and allot five minutes for each question—two minutes to prepare, and three minutes to present the argument. Teams will have to work fast. Use the following points of argument, or make up your own.

- Are youth wise or smart enough to make a difference in people's lives?
- Are youth dependable enough to make a difference in people's lives?
- Are youth experienced enough to make a difference in people's lives?
- Do youth have what it takes to get people's attention?
- Are youth old enough to make a difference in people's lives?
- Do youth have the necessary resources to make a difference in people's lives?
- Do youth have the concern and love to make a difference in people's lives?
- Do youth have the necessary skills to make a difference in people's lives?

After every team has presented its arguments, use the following for open discussion:
- Which side had the most convincing argument? Explain.
- Why do you agree or disagree with their argument?
- For what reasons would God choose a pre-teen or a teenager to make a difference in the world?

After the debates, explain that God called twelve-year-old Samuel to begin making a difference in his world. Though Samuel was very young, God saw a great deal of potential in him and demonstrated unconditional commitment to Samuel. Interestingly, there is another word for God's remarkable unconditional commitment. The Bible calls it love. Tell the youth that regardless of their age, God is unconditionally committed to them, too. God loves and trusts us enough to call everyone to a life of service—this includes clergy and other church leaders and the laity. Also mention that often in the New Testament, the Greek word *agape* was originally used to convey the essence of true Christian love—the type of love we share because of God's presence in our lives. Stated simply, *agape* is unconditional commitment—it begins with a sense of value in someone or something, and it grows as one begins to treasure this person as a valued gift of God. Perhaps the ultimate expression of unconditional commitment is found in 1 John 3:16-18. Read this passage aloud and ask: "Do you love anyone that much? Love finds a way of helping others in need, regardless of their circumstances or background. Love is characterized by action, not empty words."

Discussion
- What indications are there that God questioned Samuel's capabilities or qualifications for service?
- What indications are there that Samuel or Eli questioned Samuel's readiness for service?
- What was the final outcome?
- Based on your interests, gifts, and graces, what might God be calling you to do? At home? At school? At church? In your community? As a career?
- How can you most effectively demonstrate God's love to others? (Give examples.)
- What can your youth group do to demonstrate God's love to others?
- What can you do this week to demonstrate God's love?
- How do you show love for your family members, friends, and others?
- Who is someone you know who needs to know he or she is loved?
- What specific plan can you make this week to demonstrate love to him or her?

Their Turn

Choose at least one of the following activities to give your youth their turn at putting love into action. Use the activities to teach the youth that loving someone in terms of service means more than just saying "I love you and care about you." When you love someone enough to serve them, your actions carry the same weight as your words. And to take it a step further, when you think about serving someone where language barriers are an issue (for example, on a mission trip in a Spanish-speaking country), actions speak volumes when words aren't sufficient enough to express how you feel. **Remember—always debrief.**

Love Defined

Write the following love phrases (and any others you might think of) on newsprint and post them on the wall around the room.

- I love my cat.
- I love math.
- I love my friends.
- I love God.
- I love pizza.
- I love my boyfriend or girlfriend.
- I love my parents.

Say something like, "*Love* is one of those elusive words that's very hard to define. Today, it's often used so casually that it's hard to believe that anyone ever understands what we're trying to say!" Ask the youth take a look at all the phrases posted around the room. Then say, "We 'love' everything, don't we? Or do we? What are we really trying to say?" Go around the class and ask the youth to rephrase the statements without using the word *love*. Answers will vary, but here are some possible responses:

- I'm extremely attached to my cat.
- I do well in math.
- I like my friends a lot.
- I try to honor God.
- I prefer or enjoy pizza.
- I'm infatuated with my boyfriend.
- I try to respect my parents.

Debriefing
Have the youth write their answers on the board or newsprint.
- Which of these statements would you consider to be an expression of true love?
- What do you think true love is?

"Too-Young Yolanda" Comic Strip

Bring out plenty of large sheets of paper and colored markers and divide the youth into small groups. Read the following scenario to the class. Give them a ten minute time limit to create a "Too-Young Yolanda" comic strip based on the following dilemma. Set this rule—the cartoons have a three-panel, five-word maximum. In other words, they can't depend on a long dialogue box to make Yolanda's point. Afterwards, give each group a chance to explain their concept and answer questions. Post the cartoons on the wall.

Dilemma: Yolanda loves the small church she attends, but she hasn't been given much encouragement to express her love for the church. Unfortunately, certain people and prevalent attitudes have led her to believe "she's too young" or "not very capable" of making a significant difference at her church. "Church is the place where adults make all of the important decisions," she believes. Sadly, she feels pushed to the sidelines of service. And she's frustrated because she wants to join the team on the field.

Debriefing

- What types of influences might lead someone like Yolanda to believe she can't or shouldn't express her love for God and the church?
- What would need to change for her to feel confident about demonstrating her love for the church in acts of service?
- What would you say to those who have tainted Yolanda's thinking? What would you do to change people's attitudes? What would you say to Yolanda?
- How would you help her get started on a life of love and action?
- What do you love about our church?
- What excites you the most about it?
- What have you done to express your love for the church?
- What are some ways you can truly make a difference at our church?

Plan a Mission Possible!

1. Provide free babysitting at your church. For example, one church provides free babysitting while young parents do their Christmas shopping. They call it Santa's Helpers. Other babysitting ideas include Back to School Babysitting while parents shop for their child's school clothes or Summertime Saints, which gives parents a break in the middle of the summer. The possibilities are limitless.
2. Many churches provide some sort of financial support for their youth ministry, often through an annual youth budget or special fund-raising projects. Some do both. As a way of thanking the church for its support, offer 2-3 hours of free car washes for church members. Advertise it in the church newsletter and make announcements on Sunday morning. Don't take any money. Treat it as a gift of love.
3. Find several odd jobs to do around the church. It could include filling the pew racks with sharpened pencils, trimming shrubs, planting flowers, pulling weeds, painting a swing set, picking up trash outside or taking things to the dumpster. Ask one of the staff members for suggestions, if necessary. If you decide to do any painting or landscaping, get permission first! Try to do something that the church really needs to have done. Do it as a gift of love.

Closing

Sing together "One in the Spirit" (also known as "They Will Know We Are Christians By Our Love") or "Take My Life, and Let It Be." Read at least one of the following "Vital Verses" aloud. Remind the youth that they can find other "Vital Verses" in their *Mission Mania: Crazy to Serve* student guides. End with prayer.

NOTES

Vital Verses

Vital Verse

David said further to his son Solomon,
"Be strong and of good courage, and act. Do not be afraid or dismayed;
for the Lord God, my God, is with you."
(1 Chronicles 28:20a)

Vital Verse

"For God so loved the world that he gave his only Son, so that everyone who
believes in him may not perish but may have eternal life."
(John 3:16)

Vital Verse

We know love by this, that he laid down his life for us—and we ought to lay down
our lives for one another.
(1 John 3:16)

A Servant's Heart

Your Goals

Teenagers will . . .
▲ Understand the concept of "servanthood"
▲ Interact with real servants (in person or on paper)

We recommend leading the session in this order:
1) Choose at least one *Start-Up* activity.
2) Do *Mission Mania in the Bible* in its entirety.
3) Choose at least one *Your Turn* activity. Never forget to debrief.
4) Do the *Closing*.

The Stuff You Need

▲ Bibles
▲ Copies of "A Simple Servant Survey" (page 33) for each person
▲ Copies of the closing benediction for this session (page 32) for each person

SUPPLIES FOR OPTIONAL ACTIVITIES
For *Electric Fence* activity (page 29)
▲ Rope or twine and stakes or tall chairs
For *A Gathering of Real-Life Servants* activity (page 30)
▲ Various refreshments
For *What Famous Folks Said About Servanthood* activity (page 31)
▲ Posterboard, chalkboard, or large sheets of paper

Start Up

Who's being served?

Use at least one of these activities to help youth understand this session's theme—that in order for us to serve others, we have to start with the heart. Once God helps us develop a servant's heart, then performing acts of service can become like second nature. Also remind the youth that practice makes perfect when it comes to service. The more we serve others, the more unselfish our hearts become, and vice versa!

Move

Arrange enough chairs in a circle for everyone. Everyone sits down in a chair. The leader calls out a description on how to move. Players who fit the description follow the instructions and change chairs. For instance, if the leader says, "Move four seats to the left if you have a driver's license," persons with a driver's license would move four seats to their left, even it that means sitting on someone's lap. The following are ideas to get you started. Be creative when instructing participants to move.
▲ Move _____ if you play on a football team.
▲ Move _____ if you are going steady.
▲ Move _____ if you own a laptop computer.
▲ Move _____ if you have been to a concert lately.
▲ Move _____ if you have seen *Titanic* (insert the name of any movie).

▲ Move _____ if you enjoy rollerblading.

▲ Move _____ if you play a stringed instrument.

This exercise will force the youth to be gracious and unselfish, especially if they're required to share their seat with several other people!

Adapted from Directions in Faith, *Spring 1988; ©1988 by Graded Press. Used by permission.*

When the game is finished, briefly get feedback from the youth. Ask:

▲ How did you feel when you were forced to share your chair? Were you embarrassed? Irritated? Did you have to swallow your pride?

Electric Fence

In this game, the youth will be forced to think about the needs of others. Success will depend on their willingness to be a servant to each other. Rope off a 15' x 15' area. Suspend the rope about four feet off the ground. Stretch the rope between stakes, tall chairs, or something similar. Place the group inside the 15' x 15' area. The only way they can escape is by going OVER the four-foot-tall fence. Don't play in an area where there are rocks, sticks, or broken glass—you don't want anyone to get hurt. If the youth are still stumped after a few minutes, tell them that it's advisable to help the larger players over.

Mission Mania in the Bible

What Exactly Is a Servant?

Choose one or more of the following stories to read. You might want to split up the reading among two or more readers. Consider having several youth act out the story as the Scripture is read.

Story #1: Exodus 1:8-10, 22-2:10; Numbers 26:59b
Story #2: Joshua 2:1-15; Joshua 6:15-25
Story #3: Acts 16:16-34

Now hand out the survey on page 33 and give everyone about five minutes to complete it.

Once everyone has completed his or her questionnaire, choose one of the following options:

Option 1: Collect the response sheets, shuffle them, and read responses without divulging anyone's identity.

Option 2: Ask for volunteers to share their answers. Leave time for questions or discussion as you go through the survey one question at a time.

Option 3: This option is paired with the "A Gathering of Real-Life Servants" activity below. Proceed with option 1 or 2. Prior to the meeting, ask your real-life servant guest(s) to fill out the questionnaire. Then use a few of their responses when you introduce them or when the Question and Answer time begins.

Take Another Look at Scripture

Ask the youth to listen for the answers to the following questions as you reread one or more of today's Scripture passages.

▲ Are there any servants in these passages? How many? Who?

▲ What leads you to believe that he or she is a servant?

- ▲ What extraordinary things did this servant say or do? What was very ordinary about him or her?
- ▲ What qualities do you admire in this person or persons?
- ▲ How did he or she help someone else? Why do you think he or she helped the other person?
- ▲ How did his or her actions affect the outcome of this story?

Now probe a little deeper with the following questions. When you talk about what makes a good servant, refer especially to the answers for Questions 4 and 5 in the Servant Survey to help explain what lies in the heart of a true servant.

- ▲ Based on today's discussion, what are some of the characteristics of a servant?
- ▲ What is a servant's greatest passion? Why?
- ▲ Who in your church or community demonstrates the characteristics of a servant? Why did you choose him or her?
- ▲ What do you admire most about this person?
- ▲ Do you consider yourself a servant? Why or why not?
- ▲ What would it take for you to become one of God's servants?
- ▲ What can your youth group do (or continue to do) to become known as servants?

Their Turn

Now give the youth a chance to explore what really makes a servant's heart pump. Choose at least one of the following activities to help them understand why service is such an integral part of a Christian's faith experience. Once the youth realize that real-life servants are in all parts of the world making a difference in the lives of those in need, they'll begin to develop their very own "heart of a servant." Your job will be to encourage the youth to be open to where they think God is leading them to serve. Keep an open heart and an open mind, and your youth will begin to find ways to serve others.

A Gathering of Real-Life Servants

Note: This activity takes a small amount of planning.

Invite to your Mission Mania session up to five church members or community leaders who are well-known for their faithful Christian service. Choose a variety of servants: your congregation's senior usher, an HIV/AIDS ministry leader, an effective Sunday school teacher, the director of a local ministry to the homeless, a counselor to victims of abuse, and so forth.

The format is up to you. Have the speaker(s) give a presentation, which is more formal; or participate in a roundtable discussion, which is more informal. Whichever method you choose, give the guest(s) the following questions in advance, in addition to asking one of the guests to prepare a service-oriented prayer for this session's closing. Consider getting volunteers from the youth group to ask these questions as part of the program:

- ▲ What is your main "gift of service" to the church or community? How long have you done this?
- ▲ Talk briefly about what this ministry is and what it does.
- ▲ What's the funniest thing that ever happened while you were serving God?
- ▲ What is the most memorable time that you served God?
- ▲ What are the things you most enjoy about serving others? How has God touched you the most?
- ▲ How is serving God an expression (or an outgrowth) of your Christian faith?
- ▲ What advice would you give to teenagers trying to make a difference in today's world?
- ▲ What would you like to see the teenagers doing as servants?
- ▲ Do you have any words of wisdom for us?
- ▲ Summarize your feelings about serving others in one statement.

NOTES

Remember: these questions are suggestions. Add any other questions you can think of, making sure you encourage the youth to formulate and ask their own questions during the presentation.

Reception Option: Once the presentation or discussion has concluded, have an informal reception with an assortment of refreshments. Think about decorating the room too. This will give the youth a chance to get to know the "real-life servants" on a more personal level.

Video Option: Consider videotaping the entire presentation for future use. At a later date the youth could sponsor a presentation on "servanthood in our church and community."

What Famous Folks Said About Servanthood

Post around the room the following quotations about servanthood. Use poster board, the chalkboard, newsprint, butcher paper, or whatever is most convenient. The print should be large enough to read the quotations from a distance.

"For the Son of Man came not to be served but to serve, and to give his life a ransom for many." —Jesus Christ (Mark 10:45)

"Everybody can be great. Because anybody can serve . . .You only need a heart full of grace, a soul generated by love." —Martin Luther King, Jr.

"Whoever wants to be first must be last of all and servant of all." —Jesus Christ (Mark 9:35).

"As children of light we prepare ourselves to become true martyrs, people who witness with their whole lives to the unlimited love of God. Giving all thus becomes gaining all. " —Henri J.M. Nouwen (*The Return of the Prodigal Son,* by Henri J.M. Nouwen; DOUBLEDAY, a division of Random House, Inc., 1992; page 122).

"What is faith worth if it is not translated into action?" —Gandhi

"An individual has not started living until he can rise above the narrow confines of his individualistic concerns to the broader concerns of all humanity." —Martin Luther King, Jr.

Divide the youth into groups of four to six persons. Ask each group to answer the following questions based on the quotations posted around the room.

▲ Why is service such a big deal?
▲ Based on these quotations, what is service or servanthood?
▲ Is "serving" a negative or positive concept? Why?
▲ What does it mean when you perform service with the wrong attitude or for the wrong reasons?
▲ Each of the authors seems to be speaking with great intensity, clarity, and certainty. Why do you think that is possible?
▲ Besides service or servanthood, what *one* word ties all of these quotations together? Explain your response.
▲ What do you suppose each author would say if posed the question, "What is the great secret of service?"
▲ Why do you think service has such a powerful effect on some people?
▲ Why do you think we don't "serve others" more often?
▲ What are the benefits to others when we serve? What are ways that God blesses us when we serve others?

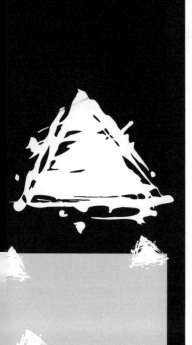

Plan a Mission Possible!

1. If you videotaped the *Gathering of Real-Life Servants* activity, use portions of the videotape during a youth group lesson on "servanthood." Considering inviting parents and others to make it an intergenerational lesson.
2. Encourage the youth to send cards of appreciation to "church servants" each year. Include both paid and volunteer servants. It could even become an annual ritual.
3. Plan and prepare a free spaghetti and salad lunch for all of the "church servants" as a way of saying "Thank you" and "You are appreciated."
4. It's possible that some of your church's great servants of the past are currently in nursing homes, have become homebound, or simply have passed the torch to a younger generation and have drifted into the shadows. As a group, visit them occasionally. Let them know they are loved, still appreciated, and not forgotten.

Closing

If you chose the *Gathering of Real-Life Servants* activity, ask in advance one of the real-life servants to prepare a closing prayer. If you chose the *What Famous Folks Said About Servanthood* activity, hand out copies of the following benediction and recite it together:

Prayer to Bless Others

The LORD bless you and keep you;
the LORD make his face to shine upon you,
and be gracious to you;
the LORD lift up his countenance upon you,
and give you peace.

(Numbers 6:24-26)

Permission granted to photocopy for use with *Mission Mania*.

NOTES

A Simple Servant Survey

Answer the following questions by placing a check mark next to your choice(s). Feel free to check more than one response for each question.

1. When you hear the word *servant,* what's the first thing that comes to mind?

    A. A slave or indentured servant
    B. A butler or maid
    C. A civil servant (example: postal worker)
    D. One of the king or queen's personal helpers
    E. Being a faithful follower of Christ

2. Being a servant is …

    A. Something with negative connotations
    B. Something to be proud about
    C. Something one does as a follower of Christ
    D. Something reserved for super Christians
    E. Something that is impossible for most people to do

3. Who among the following do you consider a servant?

    A. A Sunday school teacher
    B. Martin Luther King, Jr.
    C. Someone who ministers to the poor and homeless
    D. The person who volunteers as the part-time church secretary
    E. Someone like me

4. What makes a person a servant?

    A. The helpful things they say
    B. The unselfish things they do
    C. Their loving attitude
    D. Their willingness to put the needs of others first
    E. All of the above

5. I like the following definition of servanthood:

    A. A true follower of Christ serves others.
    B. A servant puts others ahead of his or her own agenda.
    C. Persons should serve out of love, not the desire for praise or attention.
    D. Servants are not too proud to help with the small things.
    E. Service is action, not mere words.

With 4

Passion

Your Goals

Teenagers will ...
- Reflect and talk about the things they feel passionate about
- Be challenged to develop a passion for serving others
- Grapple with hunger-related issues

We recommend leading the session in this order:
1) Choose at least one *Start-Up* activity.
2) Do *Mission Mania in the Bible* in its entirety.
3) Choose at least one *Your Turn* activity. Never forget to debrief.
   ***NOTE:* The "Aluminum Can Scavenger Hunt" activity requires being off-site and will require about two hours. If you do not have this flexibility, choose the Third World Encounter Simulation Game.**
4) Do the *Closing*.

The Stuff You Need

- Bibles
- Sheets of poster board or large sheets of paper, plus appropriate markers
- Three copies of page 40 for closing

SUPPLIES FOR OPTIONAL ACTIVITIES
For *Ping Pong Goliath* activity (page 35)
- Markers
- Paper grocery bags
- Ping pong balls
- Tub for water
- Masking tape

For *Pieces of Passion* activity (page 36)
- Lots of old magazines like *Newsweek, Time, People, Vogue,* and so forth
- Glue
- Several pairs of scissors

For *Aluminum Can Scavenger Hunt* (page 37)
- Large garbage bags
- Scale for weighing aluminum cans
- Name tags

For *Third World Encounter Simulation Game*
- See page 38 for specific supplies.

Before the class gets started, write out the following two quotations on newsprint and post them on the wall. You'll refer to them again during *Mission Mania in the Bible.*

"Your desire determines your destiny. Think of great leaders, and you will be struck by their passion: Gandhi for human rights, Winston Churchill for freedom, Martin Luther King Jr. for equality, Bill Gates for technology ... the stronger your fire, the greater your desire—the greater the potential."
(*21 Indispensable Qualities of a Leader,* by John Maxwell; Thomas Nelson Publishers, 1999; page 84).

"Caring for the poor, then, is not some kind of charity we dispense at a distance. NO, as followers of Christ, we feel their pain intensely. We cannot live separate from their dilemma any more than we can ignore the pain of our own brother or sister."
(*101 Ways Your Church Can Change the World*, by Tony Campolo and Gordon Aeschliman; copyright ©1993, Regal Books, Ventura, CA 93003).

Start Up

What's your passion?

The theme of this session is love and passion. "For teenagers?" you might shriek. Never fear! The type of love and passion you'll be addressing in this session has to do with being passionate about loving others through the gift of service. As you continue, remind the youth of the passionate faith possessed by many young Bible characters, including Samuel, the boy with the fish and loaves from the New Testament, and David, the subject of today's Bible lesson. As it may have been with David, coming to the aid of someone in need (in David's case, the Israelite army) has the potential to be a little intimidating. All it takes is a little faith and a lot of passion for helping others. Keep this session's theme in mind as you lead at least one of the following opening activities.

Ping Pong Goliath

Gather your supplies (paper grocery bag[s], ping pong balls, tub of water, marker, masking tape). Make a 2½" diameter circle on the paper grocery bag using the marker. Tape the paper bag on a wall at least 8' high (9-10' if you have the room). Put the ping pong balls in a tub of water. Then have each youth throw a ping pong ball and try to hit inside the circle. The balls should leave a slight water mark on the paper bag—in case some youth claim to hit inside the circle when they don't. With a larger group, you might need several bags, tubs, and ping pong balls.

When you finish, be sure to mop up any excess water.

This game demonstrates the difficulty David might have faced in trying to sling a stone to hit Goliath's forehead.

Train Wreck

This very active indoor game is a lot of fun. Arrange chairs in two parallel rows. Space the rows about 8-10 feet apart. Set up enough chairs for everyone, except one. That person is "it." The object of the game is to find a seat and not to become "it." The game can begin with "it" saying something like: "Everyone with blond hair, Train Wreck!" Once said, everyone with blonde hair has to find a new seat. The "it" person tries to get an empty seat too. The person left standing is "it." And the game continues for however long you like. Persons can say:

- Everyone with earrings on: Train Wreck!
- Everyone with blue on: Train Wreck!
- Everyone in 10th grade: Train Wreck!
- Everyone taking Algebra I: Train Wreck!
- Everyone with a March birthday: Train Wreck!

CAUTION!
When playing "Train Wreck," watch carefully to ensure that youth do not leap into chairs with so much force that they topple over backward!

The possibilities are endless. Ending your phrase with "Train Wreck" is saying "GO!" Tell your youth to avoid anything that is derogatory or dehumanizing. Also avoid choosing things that target a specific person. For example, if only one person is wearing a necklace, don't say "Everyone that's wearing a necklace." Another option is simply to say, "Train Wreck!" In that case *everyone* has to find an empty seat. In this case lateral movement (moving to the chair next to you) is not allowed; players *must* cross over to the other side to find an empty chair. When everyone is seated in the discussion area, say something like, "I noticed that several of you were very passionate about this game. What does it mean to have passion for something?" Give them an opportunity to respond.

Mission Mania in the Bible

David and Goliath: Approaching a Problem with Passion

1 Samuel 17:1-51

Ask several of the youth to read consecutive sections of the Scripture aloud from a contemporary translation. Then proceed immediately to the "Pieces of Passion" activity.

Pieces of Passion

Look up the word "passion" in the dictionary and read the definition aloud. To avoid getting sidetracked, read only the definitions that equate passion with overwhelming enthusiasm or intense conviction. Now divide the teenagers in groups of four to six persons. Give each group glue, scissors, a piece of poster board, and several magazines. Ask them to create a collage containing the things their individual team members are most passionate about (at least one passion per person should be represented in the collage). If creating a collage is not desirable, ask the youth to create a mural or wall of graffiti (using newsprint or butcher paper) containing all of their passions. Give them 10-15 minutes to complete this project. As the teams finish, tape the collections on the wall. Ask a representative of each team to talk about the team's passions. Allow time for comments and questions.

Take Another Look at Scripture

Read aloud the John Maxwell quotation. Remind the youth that following his passionate battle against Goliath, David was well on his way to becoming a great political and spiritual leader. Divide the group up into pairs and invite them to present their own modern-day David and Goliath stories. Tell them they only have two requirements—their contemporary David must be a person who is financially disadvantaged and their Goliath should represent a problem that someone who is poor is likely to confront. For example, their Goliath could symbolize hunger, lack of warm clothing, an angry bill collector, getting evicted from an apartment, and so on. Consider having art supplies available in case they want to get really creative. After the performances, ask these questions:

- What was David passionate about? How do you know?
- How is David's passion different from or the same as the passion you feel?
- How is the object of David's passion different from or the same as the things you're passionate about?
- What made David so passionate about addressing the problem of Goliath?
- What did David say that convinced you that he knew he could do something quite remarkable in God's name? Explain.

Now read the quotation from Tony Campolo.
- What can you do that's remarkable for God?
- How are you passionate about helping others for God?

Encourage your youth to imagine persons in need as members of their own families. This will help them understand such issues as homelessness and poverty on a more personal level. Also tell them that they're likely to become progressively more passionate about serving God each time they serve others in God's name. Ideally, serving others eventually will lead to a long-term commitment to service.

NOTES

Their Turn

Now it's time for the youth to have a turn at being passionate for God. Choose at least one of the following activities to help the youth experience life from the perspective of a person who is disadvantaged or in need. Your goal will be to help ignite their passion and establish a lifelong commitment to helping others. One way to do this is by being passionate yourself; inspire by example. Don't forget to debrief; it's essential.

Aluminum Can Scavenger Hunt

PLEASE NOTE: **This activity may require being off-site and will require about two hours. If you do not have this flexibility, choose the Third World Encounter Simulation Game.**

Make sure you have the large garbage bags and the scales for weighing them ready beforehand. If you to go to a nearby business to weigh the aluminum, make sure they know you're coming. You'll also need additional adults to accompany the small groups. (90-120 minutes)

Ask the youth if they have ever seen persons in your community collecting aluminum cans. Considering they usually pick up only a few cans at a time, ask them to guess how long it takes to fill a large garbage bag. Some people collect cans to get enough money for food. Tell them they're going to discover what it's like to collect aluminum cans for food money. The goal of this exercise is to explain that this method of obtaining money is much more difficult than it looks.

Instructions:
- Ask one or two youth to call several recycling companies in your community and get the best price per pound for scrap aluminum.
- Ask a different teenager to call a local fast food restaurant and get the exact price of a value-priced meal.
- Make sure every person has a name tag.
- Divide the teenagers into groups of five or six persons (including at least one adult per group).
- Provide each group with a large garbage bag.
- Go to a neighborhood and have each group go door to door asking for scrap aluminum cans. Don't pick through trash or dumpsters. Though persons who are poor may do this, your neighbors or police might not appreciate it. If you're concerned about visiting strangers, go to church members' homes instead. The goal is to collect enough money to buy every participant one value-priced meal from the local fast food restaurant.
- At each home introduce yourselves and tell them the proceeds of this project will help feed the hungry in your community.
- Give everyone a chance to "ring the bell" and speak on behalf of the group, but don't force anyone. Give the groups around one hour to complete this project. Weigh the aluminum cans.
- Determine the worth of the aluminum cans based on the best price available. Now divide the dollar value of the cans by the total number of participants. Determine whether the per-person amount is enough to buy everyone in the group one value-priced meal? Likely the amount is far from adequate.
- Sell the aluminum cans from your scavenger hunt and take the proceeds to your group's favorite charity (take the money in person—don't send cash). Try to choose a food pantry, soup kitchen, or another group that helps to feed the hungry. If you don't collect very many cans, some of the youth and adults might want to "chip in" one to two dollars per person to help.

Debriefing (the last 30 minutes):

Find a quiet and comfortable place to talk about your experience. Don't force anyone to speak. Some teenagers may simply want to watch, listen, and think. Others won't mind sharing their thoughts and feelings. Without allowing any one person to dominate the debriefing, ask for volunteers (teenagers and chaperons) to respond to the following.

1. What did you see and experience? Talk about what you said and did and the people you encountered.
2. What did you enjoy about collecting aluminum cans? How did it make you feel? Comfortable or uncomfortable? What about this experience would make you want to try it again? How would you feel if you were required to collect cans for a living?
3. How did the neighbors respond to the aluminum can scavenger hunt? What was the most memorable thing that someone said to you?
4. How do you suppose it made them feel to help? How did it make you feel?
5. Because of this experience, what are some of the things you learned about God? About other people? About yourself?
6. How has today's project changed your attitudes about poverty, homelessness, the elderly, your stereotypes? How has it stretched your faith? What other attitudes has it changed?
7. What do you think it would be like to depend on collecting cans for enough money to buy food each day?
8. Because of your experience with this activity, what is something you may notice now that you've never noticed before?
9. What's one thing you want to remember about today's experience?
10. What can we do as a youth group to help the hungry?

Third World Encounter Simulation Game

Objective: Get everything the family needs to survive for 24 hours. Encourage the youth to see life from the perspective of a person who is disadvantaged. "Wearing someone else's shoes" for just a moment can be enough to transform a long-held perspective or opinion. *Note:* Larger groups may create multiple living quarters if necessary. Larger groups also will need to adjust supplies accordingly.

Supplies:
100 pennies
Enough dry beans for 26 cups
Enough uncooked white rice for 26 cups
8 folding chairs
2 medium size bowls
1 small bowl
1 bottle of aspirin or candy to represent aspirin
1 small folding table
1 measuring cup

Create a living space for the two groups as follows:

Group A Living Space for a *Maximum* of Five Persons
With tape or rope, measure out a living space of 20 feet by 15 feet. This living space should include 80 pennies, 25 cups of dry beans, 25 cups of rice, 2 medium bowls (for the food), 1 card table, 1 measuring cup, 1 bottle of aspirin and 8 folding chairs.

Group B Living Space for a *Minimum* of Seven Persons, Not to Exceed Ten Persons
With tape or rope, measure out a living space of 7 feet by 15 feet. This living space should include 20 pennies, 1 cup of dry beans, 1 cup of rice, 1 small bowl (for the food), and no chairs.

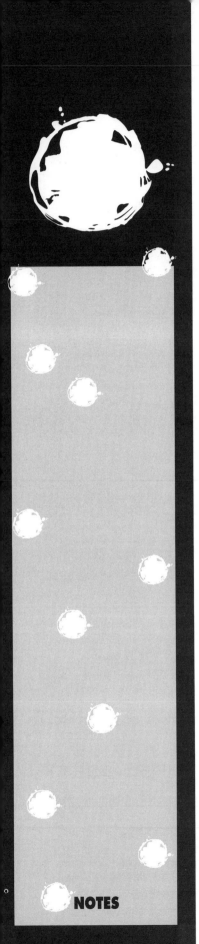

NOTES

What Everyone Needs to Know About Group A
1. The family consists of a father, a mother, and three children.
2. They have been wealthy all of their lives.
3. They don't like living close to persons who are poor. They often refer to the poor in a derogatory manner. They often treat them as a nuisance to society.

What Everyone Needs to Know About Group B
1. The family consists of a father, a mother, a sick grandmother, the father's brother and sister-in-law, and up to five children.
2. They have lived in poverty all of their lives and have learned how to "get by."
3. The parents have little education or job training; therefore their wages are quite low.
4. The grandmother needs to sleep on a bed. She is in poor health. To maintain her strength, she needs food two to three times each day. She also has to take aspirin several times a day for pain.
5. The sister-in-law is seven months pregnant. She needs a bed to sleep on. She also needs nourishing meals each day.

Third World Encounter Guidelines

*   Each group needs to select a "head of the household."
*   Set a time limit (preferably 45-60 minutes).
*   As the game begins, groups should develop a plan. For example, Group A needs to develop a strategy for dealing with Group B, while Group B needs to figure out how to ask Group A for assistance.
*   Bartering is allowed so families can get what they need. Members can either trade goods or services, or buy what they need. For example, someone can offer to shine someone else's shoes for a few pennies (or for some food).
*   The head of the household should negotiate on behalf of the group.
*   Ideally, each person should receive one cup of food per meal.
*   Each chair represents a bed for one person.
*   All supplies must be kept within the living area.
*   Trespassing is illegal.
*   There is no fixed cost of beans or rice. Get the best price you can.
*   Sleeping arrangements should be worked out within each living area. Youth should be prepared to show where each person would sleep.
*   Each participant should have one role. In other words, no one should have to represent more than one family member.

Debriefing. At the conclusion of the simulation game, gather to discuss the following:
1. What were your impressions of this activity? How did it make you feel?
2. What did you learn about Group A? Group B?
3. Was there enough food and medicine for the sick grandmother? The children in Group B? The parents and other adults in Group B? Why or why not?
4. Did group A have enough food? Why or why not?
5. Discuss whether the sleeping arrangements were suitable for everyone.
6. What was Group A's plan? Explain how well they were able to stick to their plan. What, if anything, did they give to Group B? How did giving or not giving make them feel? How easy or difficult did Group A make the task of bartering?.
7. What was Group B's plan? Explain how well they were able to stick to their plan. Did they resort to stealing? Did they attempt anything else illegal for food or money?
8. The mission for each group was to get what was necessary to survive for 24 hours. Explain how each group was able to accomplish this mission?
9. What did you learn about poverty by participating in this game? What did you learn about human nature?
10. What can your group do to address the problem of hunger in your community?

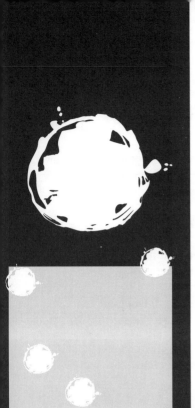

Plan a Mission Possible!

1. Using one of the suggestions in the "ideas" section of this manual (page 56), plan a firsthand encounter with poverty. Visit or volunteer (individually or as a group) at a soup kitchen, clothes closet, food pantry, or night shelter.
2. As a youth group, adopt a Third-World child through an organization like World Vision or Compassion International, a needy child (anonymously) in your community through your local school counselor, or a child at Thanksgiving or Christmas through an organization like the Salvation Army.
3. Adopt a needy family, housing complex, or neighborhood. One church delivers sack lunches to needy children on the last Saturday of every month. Though the members began by simply concentrating on one apartment complex, they currently make and deliver (with vans) nearly 150 sack lunches each month. The program and passion are growing!

Closing

Get two volunteers to do the following reading. Each volunteer will need a copy. After the reading, have everyone stand in a circle and close with a popcorn prayer, in which each person offers up a one-sentence prayer. Ask one of the youth to begin the prayer; you can finish it.

READER 1:
In spite of general affluence in the industrialized nations,
the majority of persons in the world live in poverty.
In order to provide basic needs such as food,
clothing, shelter, education, health care, and other necessities,
ways must be found to share more equitably
the resources of the world.

BOTH READERS:
Increased technology, when accompanied by
exploitative economic practices,
impoverishes many persons and makes poverty self-perpetuating.

READER 2:
Therefore, we do not hold poor people morally responsible
for their economic state.
To begin to alleviate poverty, we support such policies as:
adequate income maintenance, quality education, decent housing,
job training, meaningful employment opportunities,
adequate medical and hospital care, and humanization
and radical revisions of welfare programs.

BOTH READERS:
Since low wages are often a cause of poverty,
employers should pay their employees a wage that
does not require them to depend on
government subsidies such as food stamps or
welfare for their livelihood.

NOTES

The Pursuit of Justice

Your Goals

Teenagers will ...
- Examine justice-related issues in a creative manner
- Be challenged to become an advocate of justice

We recommend leading the session in this order:
1) Choose at least one *Start-Up* activity.
2) Do *Mission Mania in the Bible* in its entirety.
3) Choose at least one *Your Turn* activity. Never forget to debrief.
4) Do the *Closing*.

The Stuff You Need

- Bibles, preferably contemporary translations or paraphrases such as The Contemporary English Version or *The Message*
- Sheets of poster board, newsprint, or butcher paper, plus appropriate markers
- For the closing activity, enough copies of the commitment prayer from Session One (page 21) for those youth ready to make a commitment to serving others

SUPPLIES FOR OPTIONAL ACTIVITIES
For *Winners & Losers Relay* activity (page 42)
- One orange and one banana for each relay team
- Toothpicks
- Life Savers™ or any similar candy in the shape of a ring.
- Enough inexpensive prizes for each member of the winning team to receive an item (candy or small knick-knacks)

For *Losers & Winners Relay* activity (page 42)
- Round balloons
- Masking tape

For *Fish and Loaves Role Play* activity (page 43)
- See page 43 for specific supplies.

For *A Video Lesson on Justice* activity (page 44)
- TV and VCR
- *To Kill a Mockingbird* video
- Optional: drinks and fresh popcorn

For *Exploring Justice Through Creative Writing* activity
- Sheets of posterboard or large paper containing justice quotations shown on page 45.

Start Up

How do I pursue justice in today's society?

Use one of the following activities to set the tone for this session—God gives Christians the responsibility to pursue justice for those in society who can't pursue it themselves. Of course, providing such basic needs as food, clothing, and shelter is important. Equally important, however, is exploring reasons why persons are poor or disadvantaged. Having a strong sense of justice often pushes us to go beyond meeting a person's immediate needs to examine systems that cause oppression and pain. It forces us to change the way our world treats people. And it causes us to examine the way we treat people too. This session will encourage youth to look at the "big picture" and to search diligently for long-term ways to transform society.

Winners & Losers Relay

Before the game begins, announce that the winning team will be given a prize. Divide the group into two teams (more if your group is large), each standing in single file. Each team gets one orange, one banana, and a Life Saver™. Give each team member a toothpick. Players must pass the items from person to person to the end of the line and back without using their hands. Pass the orange from neck to neck. Pass the banana from knees to knees. Pass the Life Saver™ from toothpick to toothpick. Any dropped items must go back to the first of the line. Naturally, the youth will assume that the fastest team will be the winner. However, at the end of the game, give the prizes to the slowest team instead. Don't explain your actions! You should get some confused looks or some heartfelt protests about being misled. Let this go on for a short time. After a few moments of listening to complaints, explain that you wanted the youth to experience injustice firsthand at the end of the game. Ask:

* Why was it unfair for the loser to be announced as the winner?
* How did it make you feel to be treated unjustly?

NOTE: This approach works with any game in which there is a clear winner and loser.

Losers & Winners Relay

Before the game begins, announce that the winning team will be given a prize. Mark off the starting line with masking tape. Divide the group into two teams (more if your group is large), each standing in single file behind the starting line. Place a chair about fifteen feet from the head of each line. Give each team member a balloon. Players must inflate the balloon behind the starting line and then run up to the chair. Next they must sit on the balloon until it pops, and then run past the starting line before the next person can begin inflating his or her balloon. The balloon must pop; simply letting the air out of the balloon is not allowed. Naturally, the youth will assume that the fastest team will be the winner. At the end of the game, give the prizes to the slowest team instead. Don't explain your actions! You should get some confused looks or some heartfelt protests about being misled. Let this go on for a short time. After a few moments of listening to complaints, explain that you wanted the youth to experience injustice firsthand at the end of the game. Ask:

* Why was it unfair for the loser to be announced as the winner?
* How did it make you feel to be treated unjustly?

NOTE: This approach works with any game in which there is a clear winner and loser.

Mission Mania in the Bible

The Fish and the Loaves: A Boy Brings About Justice

John 6:1-14

Read the Scripture aloud to the group. Then proceed directly to the "Fish and Loaves Role Play" activity.

Fish and Loaves Role Play

Divide the group into two teams. Give each team a Bible (preferably a contemporary youth-friendly translation) and ask them to write a short skit based on the story of the fish and the loaves, *from the perspective of the little boy.* Ask the first team to pay close attention to what the little boy might have **seen**; ask the second team to pay close attention to what he might have **heard.** Send each team to opposites ends of the room or to separate rooms altogether. Give them twenty minutes to prepare the script and ten minutes to rehearse, and then have them present their skits. Here are several suggestions for possible approaches each team could take: a soliloquy; a simple dialogue between two persons (for example, the boy and Jesus, or the boy and someone in the crowd); a pantomime; a radio or TV program format (including commercials); or even puppets if they are available.

Video Option: If you have access to a video camera, a TV, and a VCR, consider videotaping each performance. Half of the fun of role-playing a Bible story is watching it on tape directly after the performance or the next time the group meets.

After the performances (or after watching the taped presentations), briefly allow each team to answer possible questions. Then ask:

- What was it like to see the story through the boy's sense of sight? Through his sense of hearing? What do you think he smelled? Touched?
- Was it fair for some to have food and others to be hungry? Why or why not?

The boy with the loaves and fish had just enough food for himself and had to give it up. This doesn't seem fair. Yet Jesus performed a miracle and fed 5,000 people, one of whom was the boy himself who had just given away his lunch.

Take Another Look at Scripture

Read aloud one more time John 6:1-14. Then ask:
- What situations in Jesus' time might have existed to have that large a crowd (5,000 people) following Jesus without having food for lunch?
- Are any of these situations justice issues?
- What unjust forces keep people from having food today?
- What was different about how Philip approached the needs of the crowd and how Andrew approached their needs?
- How did Jesus approach the crowd's needs?
- How do you respond when you see injustice occurring? At home? At school? At church?

Use this time to explain that God can take a seemingly unfair situation and turn it around so people are transformed for the better. The feeding of the 5,000 was a miracle. A miracle happens every time someone unselfishly helps another person out of an unjust circumstance. While it's difficult to understand or explain why bad things happen to good people, God gives us countless opportunities to make bad situations better for persons in need.

Their Turn

Now it's their turn. Choose at least one of the following activities to help the youth explore justice on their own. Your goal will be to help them understand that seeking justice is a whole different ball game than seeking revenge. Assure them that God depends on Christians to seek justice for those persons in society who may be disadvantaged. Don't forget to debrief—it's essential.

A Video Lesson on Justice

To Kill a Mockingbird (1962) based on the book by Harper Lee. Watch the entire film before showing it to your class.

PLEASE NOTE: **This activity requires viewing and discussing the video (about two hours long). If you do not have this flexibility, choose "Exploring Justice Through Creative Writing" or "What's Justice Got to Do With It?"**

Synopsis: This film is set in a small Great Depression-era Alabama town. Siblings Scout and Jem Finch (along with their friend Del) do not remain unaffected when their lawyer father Atticus takes on the defense of Tom Robinson, a black man accused of raping a white woman.

Cautions: *To Kill a Mockingbird* contains some violence (including shooting a rabid dog) and numerous racial slurs. Send your youth home ahead of time with a parental consent form for this film if you think it is necessary.

Watch *To Kill a Mockingbird* in its entirety. Then discuss the following. Suggested responses are provided (where appropriate) to help generate discussion.

● How did this movie make you feel?
● What would you do if someone spit in your face? Why? *Possible answers include spit back, hit him or her, yell at him or her, do nothing. Most of us are completely caught off guard when confronted with inappropriate and violent behavior. As unpleasant as it might seem, every person should think ahead of time about what he or she might do in an extreme situation. Then he or she is more likely to do the right thing, like turning the other cheek and forgiving.*

NOTES

- Evidence proved that Tom was innocent. Why do you think the jury found him guilty? *The jury made the decision before the trial even got under way. They considered the accusation alone of a black man raping a white woman as proof enough to convict Tom. In keeping with the culture of the time, the all-white jury—a "jury of the accuser's peers"—could never pass a not-guilty verdict.*

- List some different ways that Tom Robinson was treated as less of a person than he really was. *1. Everyone presumed his guilt based on his color. 2. Most people didn't even consider him a man. 3. No one interviewed him prior to the trial.*

- What sort of example did the Finch family set in their community? *They acted in a just way. They were symbols of how things could be if individuals would accept one another and act appropriately.*

- How did Atticus Finch respond to the individuals who were the meanest and nastiest to him? *He turned the other cheek, and was not intimidated by those who threatened him.*

- In what ways was Atticus Christ-like? *He visited and helped the poor. He was the only person to visit Tom Robinson's family. He tried to do what was just. He understood justice and mercy and acted on it.*

(Adapted from *Reel to Real*, Volume 2, Number 3. ©1998 by Abingdon Press. Used by permission).

Allow this discussion to develop into a wider conversation about how God expects us as Christians to respond to prejudice in everyday life. Remind the youth that prejudice is not limited to race—it comes in many forms. Encourage them to contemplate their own prejudices and to explore ways to overcome racism and other hurtful biases. Some teens may even be willing to discuss their own experiences as victims or perpetrators of intolerance. One creative exercise is to have the youth imagine themselves as parents who must explain how they will prevent their own kids from becoming prejudiced.

Exploring Justice Through Creative Writing

First, write the following King and Buechner statements on poster board or newsprint and post them on the wall. Or add your own favorite quotes about justice. There are numerous books of quotations available, and the Internet is also a good place to look.

> "When evil men plot, good men must plan. When evil men burn and bomb, good men must build and bind. When evil men shout ugly words of hatred, good men must commit themselves to the glories of love. When evil men would seek to perpetrate an unjust status quo, good men must seek to bring into being a real order of justice." — Martin Luther King, Jr.

> "If you break a good law, justice must be invoked not only for goodness' sake but for the good of your own soul. Justice may consist of paying a price for what you've done or simply of the painful knowledge that you deserve to pay a price, which is payment enough. Without one form of justice or the other, the result is ultimately disorder and grief for you and everyone." —Frederick Buechner,
>
> (Excerpt from *Whistling in the Dark*, by Frederick Buechner; Copyright ©1983 by Frederick Buechner. Reprinted by permission of HarperCollins Publishers, Inc. For additional rights/territory, contact Harriet Wasserman Literary Agency, 137 East 36 Street, New York, NY 10016).

Now, get everyone's creative juices flowing by asking them to read the posted statements and consider the following questions:

- What is the main point of each quotation? What does it mean for you? As Christians, how should we respond?

- In the King quote, what does the phrase "bring into being a real order of justice" mean to you? What can we do to make a difference?

- In the Buechner quote, what does the phrase "Without one form of justice or the other, the result is ultimately disorder and grief for you and everyone" mean to you? What kind of society do we live in—Just or unjust?

Say something like, "Now that you've had a few minutes to begin thinking about justice, it's time for you to write your own quotable thought about justice." Divide the youth into two or three groups, with no more than 4-6 persons per group. Ask each group to think about what God would say about injustice in our world and then instruct them to write one of the following from God's point of view—that is, what God would say. Some groups may want to choose more than one option. Afterwards, ask each group to present their quotes, and use the questions below for further discussion.

The assignments:

A. **Write a letter *from* God.** The letter should address an injustice within our culture. Tell the groups to concentrate on one issue like prejudice (based on race, age, gender, school, grade, intelligence, or religion), political or economic injustice, or anything else the group can think of. Tell them to address what they think God's recommendation(s) or solution(s) might be.

      Example: Dear Any Church Youth Group: I have been watching your youth group with great interest and have become increasingly saddened by the way you _____. With that in mind, stop (or begin to) . . . Love, God

B. **Write an acrostic using the word JUSTICE or INJUSTICE.** In an *acrostic,* the lines are arranged in such a way that the first letters of each line, when displayed vertically, spell a word or builds on consecutive letters of the alphabet. Make sure the groups create the acrostic from God's perspective.

    Example:

        Youth are excited about helping
        Others find justice.
        Undaunted, they steam ahead
        To make sure others deserve God's justice.
        How cool is that?!

C. **Write a haiku.** *Haiku* is a Japanese style of poetry that was frequently used to bring the beauty of nature into a precise, simple form. Each haiku consists of three lines: the first line has five syllables; the second line has seven; and the third line has five again. Remind the groups to write the haiku from God's perspective.

    Example:

        Ignoring the poor, (5 syllables)
        You hurt with unconcerned eyes. (7 syllables)
        Please open your heart. (5 syllables)

Discussion:
After the creative projects have been presented, ask the following:
Ask the presenters:
● What was it like to write something from God's perspective? Explain.
● Why did you choose to write about this particular subject?
● What feeling were you trying to convey? Why?
● What information were you trying to provide? Why?

Ask the entire group:
● How does our church, your school, or our culture deal with this subject?
● What are some steps that individuals and groups can take to address this issue?

What's Justice Got To Do With It?

Discuss the following case study with the group. Remind them that issues of justice sometimes aren't crystal clear. God, can help us sympathize with victims of injustice even if we don't understand the situation.

Case Study:

Bill doesn't believe that justice exists anymore. His home was recently robbed, and a policeman was shot during a scuffle with the alleged thief. The judge dismissed the case because the policeman did not have sufficient cause to stop the alleged robber. Though he lived, the policeman will be crippled for life. On top of everything else, Bill didn't realize that his homeowner's policy had lapsed. Now he's left with the responsibility of replacing all of the stolen items himself. Bill is infuriated.

- How do you feel about this situation?
- What do you think is the main issue in this situation?
- What would you say to Bill? Explain.
- What would you say to the policeman? Why?
- What would you say to the thief? Why?
- What would you say to the policeman's wife? His kids? Explain.
- How can justice prevail in this kind of situation? If not, what would have to be different?
- What changes should be made in society so that something like this won't happen again?

(Taken from *Tension Getters Two*. Copyright ©1985 by The Zondervan Corporation. Used by permission of Zondervan Publishing House).

Plan a Mission Possible!

1. Go to the oppressed. Plan a day trip to a night shelter, a center for victims of abuse, a prison, or a Native American Reserve.
2. Examine the words you use when referring to women, persons from other countries, and others who are traditionally considered minorities. Do you tell jokes, use slang, or categorize them in ways that dehumanize them? Spend a planned time in prayer asking God to cleanse you of sexism, racism, and pride.
3. Learn more about injustice by writing such organizations as Amnesty International, 322 Eighth Avenue, New York, NY 10001. Discover ways in which you can make a difference.
4. Don't just sit there—do something. Voice your concerns about injustice. Write your senator or congressman about glaring injustices in your community or state.

Closing

Provide everyone with copies (on colored paper, heavy card stock, or decorative certificate-style paper, if you like) of the closing litany from Session One on page 21 This time, make sure the commitment section is included. In unison, read the prayer out loud. Invite those who are ready, to sign and make a commitment. Your commitment may include making specific goals to serve the community. For example, your group may decide to visit a nursing home every month for a year, pledge to sponsor a child in need through Compassion International, or commit to working at a soup kitchen at least once per quarter. The possibilities really are endless. For mission ideas, see the list of more than 100 Double M Service Ideas that begins on page 56 of this guide and on page 20 of the student guide, *Mission Mania: Crazy to Serve.*

Track #2 —
On the Go!

Your Goals

The youth will be
▲ Equipped for mission
▲ Engaged in meaningful mission experiences
▲ Encouraged to reflect on the significance of these experiences

The *Mission Mania* leader will be
▲ Given the tools to organize five separate hands-on mission experiences
▲ Provided options that will allow customizing these experiences for any youth group.

This approach to *Mission Mania* works well for those congregations who prefer to offer the youth an off-site, hands-on service experience, or who may not be conducting a Vacation Bible School or other planned summer program. Not as structured as the In-Class approach, this option may be used on five consecutive Sundays, five consecutive weekdays or weeknights, adapted for a weekend, or used in any other sequence that seems appropriate for your group.

Each session should use as its foundation a passage from Scripture. Suggested Scriptures appear on the next page. If these passages are not appropriate for your specific event, try the alternate Scriptures listed on page 50, or use other Scriptures.

On-the-Go groups can use the church or any other pre-determined location as the initial gathering place and then travel together to the service site, or they can arrange ahead of time to gather at the site itself.

Debriefing can turn an ordinary service project into an extraordinary life-transforming occasion and is a necessary part of any mission event. Debriefing guidelines are located on page 9. Debriefing is usually most effective if conducted on-site or immediately following the service event at a nearby location. If circumstances do not allow for immediate debriefing, schedule a session for a later date. **Whatever the case, do not eliminate the debriefing session altogether. It's essential!**

Remember, be creative and never hesitate to customize the experience for your specific group.

PLEASE NOTE: Be prepared to do a lot of careful planning. Keep in mind that your youth still need to feel like they have ownership in the events, so always get their input and feedback.

Five On-the-Go Sessions

1) **Build your session on Scripture.** Choose one of the Suggested Daily Scriptures below or one of the alternate Scriptures listed on page 50. Or choose another appropriate Scripture. It's essential to impress upon your youth that service and love for others have always been God-given mandates. Thus, always use Scripture as the foundation for your sessions.

2) **Choose a project.** Decide which hands-on project from the list of Double M Service Ideas (beginning on page 56) fits your group's personality. Preferably, your project should connect with the foundation Scripture. For example, if you chose Matthew 25:35-40 as your Scripture, you might choose Service Idea #77 (page 62) as a good event for your particular group.
Note: Double M Service Ideas are categorized by level of contact. Choose your event according to your group's collective experience with service. If you do not find something that fits your group, decide on a service project of your own.

On-the-Go Suggested Daily Scriptures

Use the following daily Scriptures as inspirational words of wisdom for all who are participating in the on-site service project. They are suggestions only. If you decide that any Scripture is inappropriate for your project, feel free to choose another from the list of alternate Scriptures on page 50, or choose your own.

SESSION 1 SCRIPTURE SUGGESTION
"' . . . for I was hungry and you gave me food, I was thirsty and you gave me something to drink, I was a stranger and you welcomed me, I was naked and you gave me clothing, I was sick and you took care of me, I was in prison and you visited me.' Then the righteous will answer him, 'Lord, when was it that we saw you hungry and gave you food, or thirsty and gave you something to drink? And when was it that we saw you a stranger and welcomed you, or naked and gave you clothing? And when was it that we saw you sick or in prison and visited you?' And the king will answer them, 'Truly I tell you, just as you did it to one of the least of these who are members of my family, you did it to me.'" (Matthew 25:35-40)

SESSION 2 SCRIPTURE SUGGESTION
"We love because he first loved us. Those who say, 'I love God,' and hate their brothers or sisters, are liars; for those who do not love a brother or sister whom they have seen, cannot love God whom they have not seen. The commandment we have from him is this: those who love God must love their brothers and sisters also." (1 John 4:19-21)

SESSION 3 SCRIPTURE SUGGESTION
"It will not be so among you; but whoever wishes to be great among you must be your servant, and whoever wishes to be first among you must be your slave; just as the Son of Man came not to be served but to serve, and to give his life a ransom for many." (Matthew 20:26-28)

SESSION 4 SCRIPTURE SUGGESTION
"When he saw the crowds, he had compassion for them, because they were harassed and helpless, like sheep without a shepherd." (Matthew 9:36)

SESSION 5 SCRIPTURE SUGGESTION
"He said to him, 'You shall love the Lord your God with all your heart, and with all your soul, and with all your mind.' This is the greatest and first commandment. And a second is like it: 'You shall love your neighbor as yourself.' On these two commandments hang all the law and the prophets." (Matthew 22:37-40)

Alternate On-the-Go Scriptures

Choose any of the following if you decide the Scriptures listed on the previous page are inappropriate for your particular project.

"If there is among you anyone in need, a member of your community in any of your towns within the land that the Lord your God is giving you, do not be hard-hearted or tight-fisted toward your needy neighbor. You should rather open your hand, willingly lending enough to meet the need, whatever it may be." (Deuteronomy 15:7-8)

"He sat down, called the twelve, and said to them, 'Whoever wants to be first must be last of all and servant of all.'" (Mark 9:35)

"The greatest among you will be your servant. All who exalt themselves will be humbled, and all who humble themselves will be exalted." (Matthew 23:11-12)

"In everything do to others as you would have them do to you; for this is the law and the prophets." (Matthew 7:12)

"We know love by this, that he laid down his life for us—and we ought to lay down our lives for one another." (1 John 3:16)

"Give liberally and be ungrudging when you do so, for on this account the Lord your God will bless you in all your work and in all that you undertake. Since there will never cease to be some in need on the earth, I therefore command you, 'Open your hand to the poor and needy neighbor in your land.'" (Deuteronomy 15:10-11)

"Share your food with everyone who is hungry." (Isaiah 58:7a [CEV])

Track #3 — Weekend/Retreat

Use this approach if you and your youth prefer an overnight or weekend hands-on mission experience. This approach can stand alone or be paired with the two other approaches in various combinations. For example, plan a one-time special mission event, or culminate a five-day VBS In-Class *Mission Mania* experience with a weekend out-of-town service retreat. The possibilities are endless!

Of the three *Mission Mania* approaches, this one requires the most planning.
See the information below for things to remember if you decide to plan a weekend service project. The Weekend/Retreat approach works best when several mission events are experienced over the course of the retreat. Larger groups will need to divide into smaller service teams that either work at different tasks in the same facility or that travel to different projects within the same city. Beginning on page 52, you'll find suggestions for helping you have a successful weekend service retreat, and a sample schedule.

First Things First

The initial approach to a weekend/retreat-style mission event is basically identical to the On-the-Go method.

1) **Build your service project on Scripture.** Choose one of the Suggested Daily Scriptures on page 49 or one of the alternate Scriptures listed on page 50. Or choose your own appropriate Scripture. It's essential to impress upon your youth that service and love for others have always been God-given mandates. Thus, always use Scripture as the foundation for your sessions.

2) **Choose a project.** Decide which hands-on project from the list of Double M Service Ideas (beginning on page 56) fits your group's personality. Preferably, your project should connect with the foundation Scripture. For example, if you chose Matthew 25:35-40 as your Scripture, you might choose Service Idea #77 (page 62) as a good event for your particular group.
Note: Double M Service Ideas are categorized by level of contact. Choose your event according to your group's collective experience with service. If you do not find something that fits your group, decide on a service project of your own.

Preparing for a Weekend/Overnight Service Retreat

Plan Ahead

To have a successful *Mission Mania* event (especially if your group is traveling), plan early. There will be much to do. Many of the components require advance work.

Get Permissions and Information

You need not only your church's permission to go on a *Mission Mania* trip, but you will also need written permission from parents to take their youth on the trip. You'll need basic information and permission for medical attention in the event of an emergency. If your trip is an extensive one out of the country, you may need appropriate travel documents, such as passports and visas. If your church has legal advisers available, check with them before making the trip. Find out what your church insurance does and does not cover. Many policies are not valid outside of the country in which they're issued. Determine if additional insurance is necessary.

Be Safety Conscious

Though it goes without saying, avoid dangerous or precarious situations. Review safety rules regarding tools, and investigate medical facilities in the area of your project. Take along plenty of first aid supplies. See page 64 for a list of what to include in a good first aid kit. Train as many people—including youth—as possible in first aid procedures. This skill is one of the greatest gifts you can give a youth group.

Communicate

Communicate with youth, leaders, parents, church officials, and people at your project site. Don't assume people know what is supposed to happen. Talk about it and put it in writing. Publicize your mission experience to your congregation and enlist their support. Few things inspire people more than seeing young people getting involved in ministry and service. Being certain that people know about your trip can have a deeply positive impact upon the congregation. In addition, many people with skills you will need may offer to train your youth or accompany your group. Others may offer supplies, tools, financial contributions, or prayers. All of these are necessary to make the trip a success.

Prepare for Emergencies

Take extra funds to cover emergencies. Distribute group funds among several people rather than letting one person carry all of the money. Use traveler's checks if practical. Have a list of emergency phone or fax numbers.

Use Good Judgment

Avoid sleeping, travel, and other living arrangements that might be vulnerable to interpretations of physical or sexual abuse. Check your church's or denomination's recommendations concerning this matter.

Use an Organization

Many groups have had a great deal of experience in putting together mission experiences for youth. Take advantage of their expertise. They can save you a lot of time, effort, or money.

Prepare Your Group

Make sure you discuss cultural differences that may become obvious once the service event is under way. For example, persons in the Caribbean tend to prefer to be called nationals, not natives. Many cultures expect a cordial greeting before answering a question. Especially if your group is traveling outside the US, do everything you can to overcome the "Ugly American" perception sometimes held by persons in other cultures. In addition, planning a day project using skills that you will need on your *Mission Mania* trip will help everyone feel more comfortable. Many young people may not be familiar with carpentry, painting, roofing, or other types of manual labor. Show your youth how to do these things before you go!

Fundraising

The simple truth is that people often are much more committed to participating in a project when it has a cost. If your youth invest themselves in fundraising projects, their enthusiasm for and commitment to a *Mission Mania* event will grow.

Be Flexible

Once you have arrived at your project site, be aware that things may change. Materials may not arrive on time, or equipment may malfunction. Don't spend time worrying about what you cannot fix. Find something else to do. There will likely be plenty of things to accomplish.

Celebrate, Educate, and Motivate

Celebrate your successes within your own group, within the congregation, and within the community. After returning from a project, enlist some of your youth, perhaps with some adult assistance, to put together programs for Sunday school classes and other church and community groups. Consider concluding your presentations by offering people an opportunity to get involved with local projects where there is great need.

Debrief

Never forget to debrief; it's essential! Debrief daily and at the end of the entire event. This is the one step *not* to overlook. See page 9 for why debriefing is so important.

Follow Up

Post photographs or show videotapes of the event. Follow-up projects can capitalize on the enthusiasm generated by the service retreat. As a group, make sure you thank everyone who helped. Send notes and letters to your hosts, sponsors, and adults who have committed their time.

Take a Pre-Trip

Whether your weekend service project is two blocks or two states away, it's a good idea to visit the project site before taking a group. If your event is not conducted by an organization, such as a well-established work camp, don't even think of taking youth until you have thoroughly checked it out! Taking a pre-trip may seem like an unnecessary expense, but it will be some of the best money you'll spend.

A pre-trip allows you to:

◆ Determine the safety of the area.

◆ Note living accommodations.

◆ Determine which supplies need to be brought by the group and which can be obtained on the premises.

◆ Establish important personal contacts.

◆ Make more detailed plans for your *Mission Mania* event.

◆ Eliminate anything that could result in "unwanted surprises."

Take plenty of photos or slides on your pre-trip. They will help generate enthusiasm from youth, parents, and the congregation. Use the pictures to get people excited, to enhance your fundraising efforts, and to explain some details to the youth as they prepare. **Give the photos from your pre-trip and photos of your youth to members of the congregation.** Ask them to pray daily for the youth and the people they'll be serving. Make the request as a part of your congregations' send-off in worship, or ask the youth to choose someone and personally deliver the request and a photo.

Sample Overnight Weekend Schedule

The schedule that follows is merely a sample based on service projects selected from the list of Double M Service Ideas on page 56. You may need to alter this schedule based on your group's interests and available ministry sites. *Be creative and offer several types of mission experiences during the weekend.* Make sure you do plenty of planning ahead, and debrief at the end of each day!

The size of your group (and the facility you are visiting) will dictate the number of service teams needed. Larger churches will want to divide their group. It might be necessary to scatter and have teams working in several locations, or to have several teams doing different things in the same facility.

Saturday Morning

8:00 AM   Meet at church (or other previously established location) to load equipment and overnight bags.

8:30 AM   Have your initial briefing, describing the first project, what to expect, and special instructions. Pray as a group before leaving for the first site.

9:30 AM   Arrive at local soup kitchen. Help prepare and serve the noon meal. Do odd jobs, cleaning, and other tasks as needed.

Saturday Afternoon

Noon	Eat lunch at soup kitchen. Discuss that morning's project.
1:00 PM	Hold your briefing for second and third stops. Travel to second site.
1:30: PM	Help sort food and clothing at a food bank or clothes closet. Do cleaning, filing, stocking, or other work as needed.
3:00 PM	Leave for third work site. Discuss the day's activities on the way. Stop for snacks and drinks, or hand out refreshments on the way.
3:30 PM	Do yard work for someone in need: trim shrubs, edge the sidewalk, clean up. Tell him or her in advance that you're coming. Don't ask for or take any donations for your work. Explain that it is a gift of love!
	Note: *If your group is large, divide into teams to cover more than one yard. Make sure you gather at a central spot before leaving for the evening meal.*
5:30 PM	Leave for evening meal. Discuss the day's events. Hold the briefing about the next work site.

Saturday Evening

6:45 PM	Leave for your final destination. Hold "Game Night" at a night shelter. Give inexpensive prizes to the winners. Do cleaning or other odd jobs as needed.
8:15 PM	Depart for your overnight location, where you'll lead the day's final debriefing.
8:45 PM	Have the final debriefing. Leave the rest of the evening open for recreation.
11:30 PM	Get ready for bed.

Sunday Morning

8:00 AM	Eat breakfast.
9:00 AM	Before departing, hold a briefing about the church, their style of worship, their ministries, and what to expect when your group goes to visit.
9:30 AM	Worship with an inner-city church that serves persons who are disadvantaged.
Noon	Eat lunch, have the final debriefing and evaluation of the weekend, and depart for home.

Double M Service Ideas: 100+ Ways to Make a Difference

> ## "If anyone wants to be first, he must be the very last, and the servant of all."
>
> *Mark 9:35*

If you're having difficulty thinking of ways to serve your congregation or your community, challenge your youth to develop a mission-oriented purpose, vision, or dream statement. Make sure it's compatible with the policies, procedures, and purpose of your church. Once they have a mission-oriented purpose you will be better able to determine which of the Double M Service Ideas below best fits your group.

The suggestions are grouped according to "contact level." In other words, some events require extensive personal interaction with the recipients while others involve minimal contact. If your group is full of brand-new Mission Maniacs, then it's advisable to start small and graduate to more complex, highly relational service opportunities. Make sure you have a good idea of your group's overall "personality" before you choose an activity. Remember that all of these suggestions can be customized to fit your group. Here are some guidelines to get you started:

▲ Select projects that are suitable for you, your youth group, church, and community. For example, if yours is an inner-city church, you probably wouldn't choose Idea #88—Take a mission trip to the inner city. Do something that you are truly excited about.

▲ If your group has no previous mission experience, it is advisable to begin with ideas from the "No Contact" or "Low Contact" lists since "High Contact" projects tend to be highly relational. If your group is more experienced, this suggestion may not be applicable.

▲ Service events lose their "servant edge" when transformed into a fundraiser. Therefore, keep the projects free of cost to the recipients.

▲ An event that involves "No Contact" in one setting might be "Low" or "High Contact" in another. In other words, unexpected variables may affect the degree of contact from week to week, or community to community. Be prepared for that possibility.

TYPES OF SERVICE EVENTS BASED ON LEVEL OF CONTACT

NO CONTACT
Participants usually have no or very minimal direct interaction with the recipients.
Example: Sorting food at a food pantry

LOW CONTACT
Participants have minimal interaction with the recipient.
Example: Mowing an elderly person's yard

HIGH CONTACT
Participants have high amount of personal, often one-on-one interaction with the recipients.
Example: Providing a daily VBS for underprivileged kids

Note: These categories are for guidance only and are not necessarily mutually exclusive.

"No-Contact" Service Ideas

1. **Give a special birthday tithe.** Set aside 10% of the money you receive (or 10% of the money that was spent) on your birthday to help support a soup kitchen, night shelter, abused children's center, abused women's facility, or clothes closet.

2. **Begin a Parking Meter Buddies program.** Some communities will allow your youth to assist motorists by dropping quarters into parking meters that have expired. Make sure you check before doing this one. Some groups may want to leave a calling card under the car's windshield wiper with a brief note. For example, the card might read: "The no-strings 25 cents gift of love placed in your expired parking meter was provided by the teenagers of Anywhere Christian Church, Anytown, USA."

3. **Support a Third-World child.** Financially support a Third-World child through such groups as Compassion International or World Vision. Many of these and other agencies can be researched on the Internet.

4. **Participate in the 30-Hour Famine.** This annual event helps students raise funds to help end world hunger as they become sensitive to Third World hunger issues. Learn more about it by visiting www.30hourfamine.org.

5. **Write a letter or card of encouragement.** Send it to friends, family, shut-ins, the sick, the lonely, the bereaved, absentees—anyone who you know needs encouragement.

6. **Sponsor a Third World Meal.** A meal of white rice, water and bread with a lesson on world hunger can help students become more sensitive to poverty and hunger-related issues.

7. **Prepare Final Exam Survival Kits.** Send college students Final Exam Survival Kits including such items as pencils, pens, floppy disks, snacks, exam booklets (blue books if they are used), instant coffee, pain reliever, and antacid.

8. **Get involved with Habitat for Humanity.** Depending on the policies (for example, age restrictions) of your local Habitat for Humanity affiliate, students may be able to help with such things as painting, food delivery, running errands, laying sod, and other construction-related projects.

9. **Start a Weekly Prayer Pals group.** As a group, pray weekly for local, state, national, and international mission work. Your church's denominational offices will be able to provide you with the names of people and projects needing prayer.

10. **Support local and global missionaries.** Many congregations encourage their members to be financial (and prayerful) supporters of missionaries all over the world. Contact your church's denominational offices for more information.

11. **Write those missionaries from Item #10.** Foreign and state-side missionaries are always encouraged by caring letters.

12. **Send a kid to camp.** Raise funds to send a child to church camp. Give the gift anonymously.

13. **Help sort food at a food bank.** See if your local food bank or food pantry can use the help of your youth group. Be sure to call in advance to schedule a date and time with them.

14. **Plant trees or flowers in the park.** Call your city hall to receive permission and instructions. Some cities may even provide the trees or flowers.

15. **Paint the "jungle gym" or swing set at the park.** Call your city hall to receive permission and instructions. Some cities may even provide the paint.

16. **Sponsor a child in need at your local elementary school.** Anonymously sponsor a needy child (for example, provide clothing, school supplies, food) through a local school. Begin by calling the school counselor's office. He or she should be able to point you in the right direction.

17. **Plant flowers at church.** Spruce up the church by planting flowers. Talk to the pastor about gaining permission (and possibly even the supplies) to begin this project.

18. **Participate in an Earth Day celebration.** Earth Day is an annual event held usually in April. Your participation could include (but is not limited to) a special youth group lesson, guest speaker, planting flowers, or planting a tree. Be creative!

19. **Adopt a Highway.** Countless communities have Adopt-a-Highway programs in which community groups keep a section of local highway neat and free of trash. Before beginning, consult your local highway patrol or city hall. They may assign you a specific section of the road or highway.

20. **Write letters to inmates.** Send cards or letters of encouragement or provide Christmas gifts to their children through your local jail or prison or through such groups as Prison Fellowship. Use caution before providing your last name, address, or phone number.

21. **Help sort clothing.** Check with your local clothes closet to see if it needs help stocking, expanding, or sorting clothing items.

22. **Collect used eyeglasses.** Donate your old eyeglasses to an organization (like the Lenscrafters® "Give the Gift of Sight" program) that distributes them to the needy.

23. **Make Care Packages for those in need.** Prepare and deliver (or mail) thoughtful Care Packages for such groups as college freshmen, prison inmates, nursing home patients—anyone who needs some encouragement.

24. **Pray for the poor, homeless, and hungry.** Set aside a special time during your youth meeting to pray specifically about these issues.

25. **Collect socks or mittens during Christmas.** Groups like the Salvation Army may appreciate gifts of new socks or mittens for children, teenagers, and adults in need. Call your local Salvation Army about the possibility of beginning this seasonal partnership.

26. **Be a Christmas Angel Tree sponsor.** Malls, banks, and care-giving organizations in many communities conduct some sort of Christmas Angle Tree project. Take one or more of their Angel Tree cards, raise the funds, and purchase and wrap the Christmas gift(s) for children or senior adults in need.

27. **Prepare school supply packets for schools in underprivileged areas.** Consult your school district offices or your school counselor's office to gain insights and information about this process.

28. **Volunteer to be church janitors for a weekend.** Spend a Saturday morning cleaning up your church. Call the church office to schedule a suitable morning for this project.

29. **Collect clothing or canned goods for local care-giving agencies.** Many clothes closets and food pantries are in constant need of ministry supplies. Call them to determine what is needed most.

30. **Have a Trash Bash.** If you are in an area that has unkempt vacant lots, spend the morning picking up trash. People will notice the difference!

31. **Sponsor a Christmas Party for Jesus.** Instead of bringing gifts for one another, ask participants to purchase, wrap, and bring gifts to be taken to a local charity. For gift ideas, many charities have "wish lists."

32. **Collect toys at Christmas for a local agency.** Typically, local agencies will know of children in need of a Christmas gift. Consult with them to see how your youth can help.

33. **Hold a paper or aluminum can drive.** Use the proceeds to help support a local night or women's shelter (or charity of your choice). Besides helping someone, you're helping the environment too!

34. **Organize a "service arm" of your youth group.** If your group gets excited about *Mission Mania,* dedicate a special aspect of your youth ministry to mission work and call it a creative name. One such youth group organizes its service projects under the name Creve Coeur Ministries. Creve Coeur is French for "broken heart." They even have special aprons sporting the Creve Coeur logo!

35. **Collect "pennies for poverty."** Everyone always has extra pennies lying around. Use the proceeds to help support a local soup kitchen, night shelter, or clothes closet.

36. **Send thank-you cards to your church's church school or Sunday school teachers and leaders.** At the start or end of the church school year, send notes of appreciation to the volunteer staff.

37. **Go on a Book Binge.** Donate brand-new children's books to your church library, the public library, an orphanage, hospital waiting rooms, or wherever they're needed. Consider donating classics, Christian bestsellers, and award-winning books.

38. **Donate a Computer.** Donate a high-quality used computer, or collect funds and donate a new computer to a low-income area school. Also consider offering classes in typing, word processing, or Internet navigating, led by interested members of your youth group.

39. **Participate in SOUPER Bowl Sunday.** On Super Bowl Sunday, collect money and canned food for local food distribution group or soup kitchens. SOUPER Bowl Sunday is a national effort and is located on the Web at *www.souperbowl.com.*

40. **Install a "Beverage Machine for Missions."** In your youth room (or suitable location) install a beverage machine and use the proceeds to support a Third-World child, a local family, or a favorite ministry. Be sure to get church approval first!

41. **Start a Pew Crew.** If someone is not already responsible for keeping the pews ready for Sunday, be in charge of keeping the pews looking nice and stocked with cards and pencils.

42. **Send Compassion Cards.** Watch your local newspaper and send cards to persons who have experienced a recent tragedy. Consider delivering them a small potted plant.

"Low-Contact" Service Ideas

43. **Shared Birthday Blessings.** On your own birthday, take a wrapped gift to someone who is shut-in, bereaved, sick, or is facing a difficult time in life.

44. **Rake Someone's Lawn.** With or without notice, rake an elderly person's lawn and leave a note saying who did it, or do it anonymously. Don't take any payment.

45. **Go on a Teen Quest.** Collect and take Christian CD's and tapes, teen magazines, board games, school supplies, teen Bibles, clothing or anything else needed to a local children's home.

46. **Create some Carnation Compassion.** Deliver free carnations (with a brief note) on any given holiday like Mother's Day, Father's Day, or Easter to a nursing home, hospital, maternity ward, home near your church, supermarket, mall, or other public place. You may need to get advance permission.

47. **Clean an elderly person's garage.** Ask your pastor, senior adult coordinator, or senior adult Sunday school teacher(s) for suggestions concerning those they think would benefit from this gift of service.

48. **Have a Blanket Blitz.** Collect blankets and deliver them to the street people on a cold night. You might even want to take sandwiches and hot drinks. ***Note:*** This requires adequate adult supervision.

49. **Take fresh-baked bread or cookies to an immigrant family.** This unexpected gift of love might start a conversation or even a new friendship!

50. **Adopt a nursing home.** Help provide magazines, fresh fruit, flowers, hygiene packets, or other supplies needed by a local nursing home. Some nursing homes are in need of used hymnals, Bibles, large-print Sunday school curriculum, and audiocassettes of sermons or curriculum. Consult your local nursing home to discover what it needs.

51. **Adopt an orphanage in your area.** Provide field trips, game and movie nights, new clothing, tutoring, or any other services needed.

52. **Throw a youth-sponsored baby shower.** Youth groups are not typically known for throwing baby showers. Maybe it's time to begin a new tradition—particularly if the parents-to-be are staff members, volunteer youth workers, or youth group members.

53. **Take cookies to a bereaved family.** Whether the cookies are homemade or store-bought, the thoughtfulness behind your gift will be a source of comfort.

54. **Take a magazine to someone in the hospital.** Spend an evening taking magazines to church members (and prospective members) who are in the hospital or recuperating at home. See if you can find out the person's favorite magazine and surprise him or her with a personalized gift!

55. **Provide care for caregivers.** Take a small gift to the nurses or nurse's aides at your local hospital (or to a specific floor or department). Include a card with the message from your youth group.

56. **Restock a hospital's waiting rooms with new magazines.** Many hospital waiting rooms are cluttered with out-of-date magazines. Call your local hospital to see if your group can restock the waiting rooms with current publications. Students may choose to purchase new magazines or ask church members to save relatively new magazines for them.

57. **Provide free "treats" at local events.** Contact the local event coordinator to see if he or she would allow your group to distribute free bottled water, sports drinks, cookies, fresh fruit, helium-filled balloons (to name a few) at their event.

58. **Organize a SickNet.** To make sure that members of your congregation who are sick do not go unnoticed, pledge to call or write them on a regular basis.

59. **Adopt a Grandparent.** Send special-occasion cards or notes, call, and talk to them at church.

60. **Become a partner-in-missions with the youth group from another congregation.** Build friendships with other youth groups within your community by attending one of their worship services, participating in a joint Bible study or activity, or working together on a joint mission project.

61. **Wrap Christmas packages at the mall.** During the week prior to Christmas, offer a free gift wrapping service in the mall. Get permission and special instructions from your local mall operator.

62. **Sponsor (which also includes cooking and serving) an evening meal for a local civic organization.** Civic groups often encourage churches (and youth groups) to sponsor one of their evening meals. Consult local civic organizations for details about their needs, policies, and schedule.

63. **Touch others by telephone.** As a group, volunteer at the telephone center for a troubled teen or crisis counseling center.

64. **Prepare a Thanksgiving basket for a family in need.** Many churches, schools, and civic groups know of persons who will not otherwise have a Thanksgiving meal. Call to see how you can help.

65. **Develop an ongoing partnership with an adult Sunday school class.** Working with their class president, schedule a jointly sponsored afternoon of mission work.

66. **Deliver kisses (chocolate ones, that is).** Around Valentine's Day or any other holiday, take a large chocolate kiss or a wrapped container of small kisses to someone in the hospital. Or distribute them free of charge (with a small note) at the mall (with permission, of course).

67. **Celebrate an Easter Basket Extravaganza.** Take Easter baskets, bags of candy, or cards to children in the hospital. Call the chaplain or the director of volunteer services for permission and instructions. This can work with just about any holiday that has kid appeal, like Halloween or Valentine's Day.

68. **Deliver Prayer Bears.** Collect new stuffed bears for the children's hospital or in your area. During Christmas, many police departments also collect toys for children. Before taking the toys to the hospital, the group should pray and ask God to bless each recipient who receives a bear. Consult the chaplain or director of volunteer services to schedule a drop-off date.

69. **Mow an elderly person's yard or trim the bushes for free.** Contact the person in advance, set an appointment to help with his or her yard work. Do it free of charge!

70. **Have a Scavenger Food Hunt.** Instead of hunting for treasure, hunt for food! Prepare a scavenger hunt list of canned and non-perishable food items. Take the collected items to a local food pantry. An adult should accompany each group of teenagers as they go door-to-door.

71. **Conduct Movie Night at a night shelter.** Hold a free Movie Night (with popcorn and drinks) at your local night shelter. Or have a Game Night.

72. **Go Christmas Caroling at a local children's hospital.** Call in advance to schedule this memorable encounter with children! You may even want to go caroling in celebration of other holidays: Easter, Thanksgiving, maybe even Groundhog's Day. Who knows? Be creative!

73. **Sponsor a free Car Wash.** Instead of using car washes simply for fund-raising purposes, set aside a couple of hours one Saturday for a free community car wash!

74. **Sponsor an Easter egg hunt.** Help kids hunt for Easter eggs at your home, the children's hospital, nursing home, children's home, night shelter, or wherever this gift of love is needed most.

75. **Prepare Prison Packs.** Prepare hygiene packs for the persons incarcerated in your local county jail (or prison). Your local jail (prison) will have instructions concerning what (and what not) to include in the packs.

76. **Start a police station/fire station ministry.** Take beverages and snacks to your local police precinct or fire station, especially during the blistering summer months. Be sure to call first!

"High-Contact" Service Ideas
Note: Most of these will require advance planning and scheduling.

77. **Volunteer at a local soup kitchen, food distribution center, or night shelter.** You will be surprised at the ways in which God touches your life, while you attempt to touch the lives of others with God's love. *The degree of contact may range between "low" and "high" contact depending on the facility restrictions and the nature of your group.*

78. **Organize a neighborhood block party.** As a ministry to the homes surrounding your church, hold a free block party complete with cookout-style food, drinks, music, games, and entertainment.

79. **Develop a pet ministry.** Sometimes known as P.A.W.S. (Pets Are Wonderful Servants), this idea involves taking well-behaved household pets (dogs, cats, birds) to a local nursing home where they can interact with the residents. Make sure you call their volunteer coordinator in advance.

80. **Sponsor a Special Day for Special Kids.** Have the youth sponsor a field trip or special day for children who are disadvantaged or handicapped.

81. **Deliver sack lunches.** Consider delivering nourishing sack lunches (perhaps on a monthly basis) to the residents of local low-income housing communities and hotels.

82. **Go on a Vacation Bible School Mission.** Conduct a youth-led VBS for a church that would otherwise be unable to host a VBS on their own. Or offer your services as volunteer VBS workers to a small struggling congregation.

83. **Go on a Barbecue Blitz.** Prepare and serve a hot plate lunch (hot dogs, chips, drinks, and dessert) for the residents of a low income housing community or hotel. The end of the month is often a good time to provide this free meal, since people's funds may be running low. Get appropriate permission, do lots of publicity, and work out all of the details in advance. *Note:* In some areas it might be more appropriate to provide a warm breakfast instead.

84. **Serve as Santa's Helpers.** Provide free babysitting so that parents of young children can go Christmas shopping.

85. **Visit someone at home, in jail, or at the hospital.** Be God's heart and hands by reaching out to others during their time of need.

86. **Develop an ongoing ministry for people unable to leave home.** Take Sunday school curriculum, large-print reading material, or sermon tapes and videos to those in your congregation who are unable to leave home. Spend time to develop a friendship with each person. It may be necessary to bring a portable tape player or TV and VCR.

87. **Start an AIDS Care Team.** Visit the homes of persons with AIDS. Shopping, cleaning, and listening might be a part of this ministry. Your local AIDS Interfaith Network will be able to help establish and coordinate this ministry.

88. **Take a mission trip to the inner-city.** Whether it's a one-day, weekend, or week-long experience, consider being a part of an inner-city mission trip experience. There are many reputable organizations that can help with this sort of event.

89. **Take small potted plants to residents of a local nursing home.** Some nursing homes prefer other types of gifts. Consult with them first.

90. **Take food and blankets to persons who are homeless.** This suggestion is quite an undertaking. Adults are required. Make sure you notify the police about this project.

91. **Start an after-school sports, latchkey, or tutoring program.** A good place to start is to consult with your pastor and local elementary schools. They'll be able to point you in the right direction.

92. **Take a mission trip with churches from your area.** Many denominations sponsor regional mission trips which typically focus on home construction or repairs, disaster relief, or poverty relief. Call your denominational offices for more information. Individual projects may range from low to high contact.

93. **Build a home with the Appalachian Service Project.** The Appalachian Service Project (ASP) helps build homes for needy persons in the Appalachian mountains. For more information, visit their web site at *www.asphome.org*.

94. **Throw a Post-Prom Party.** Sponsor a drug- and alcohol-free Post-Prom Party at a neutral location. Your high schools and local businesses might be willing to support this thoughtful event. Ask them!

95. **Host an Agape Meal.** Invite the hungry and homeless in your community to a free meal. Weigh the pros and cons of providing the meal at your church or at a neutral site. Or you might want to consider delivering it to impoverished neighborhoods or housing complexes. Due to its popularity, one inner-city church holds an Agape Meal weekly.

96. **Deliver the Sunday morning flowers to persons in the hospital.** Some churches don't know what to do with the leftover flowers from Sunday morning. If flowers go unclaimed, deliver them to someone in the hospital or to a shut-in.

97. **Volunteer to assist groups that work with persons who are developmentally handicapped.** Events such as the Special Olympics are looking for dependable and caring volunteers.

98. **Sponsor a Karaoke Night.** Invite another group within your church (children, young married couples, parents of teens, special education, senior adults) to an evening of fun. This great mission opportunity is a wonderful way to develop relationships within your church. Some churches may want to invite persons who are homeless to an evening of fun.

99. **Develop your own soup kitchen, night shelter, food pantry or clothes closet.** Many teenagers are more than willing to develop a ministry of their own. When the youth are given sufficient training and guidance, such programs can do a world of good.

100. **Have a Young-at-Heart Banquet.** Pair teenagers with the elderly to have a "date" and an evening of fun. Provide music, entertainment, a meal, and guest speaker.

101. **Become a summer camp counselor or counselor-in-training.** Depending on age requirements, many summer camps need young and energetic camp counselors and/or counselors-in-training.

102. **Encourage your teenagers to become mission volunteers.** Many denominations offer information and opportunities for volunteer mission work. Contact your denominational offices.

BONUS: **Now that your group is full of Mission Maniacs, sponsor a Super Summer of Service!** Schedule a series of one-day service projects throughout the summer.

Important Medical Information

Using Medical Release Forms

Individual liability/medical release forms are highly recommended for every mission project.
Make sure you are prepared for the possibility of injuries.

▲ See if your church already has an approved (or recommended) release form. Use it!

▲ See if your church's denominational offices have an approved (or recommended) form.

▲ Consult with area youth directors. They might have several different forms to recommend.

▲ Consult with a lawyer in your church (or community). It's better to have a form tailored to your state and local laws, and to the needs of your church.

▲ Place the completed forms in a binder and take them with you throughout the trip. You'll need to have them close to you at all times!

▲ Don't use "blanket release" forms (ones that are supposedly good for a specific period of time). General forms can be too vague and therefore too difficult to enforce. Use a new release form for every trip. Include the name of the event, date(s), the participant, and group leader.

▲ ***Use one form per person.*** Each sibling should be listed on a separate form.

▲ A good form will include blanks for insurance policy numbers, emergency phone numbers, a place to list allergies and medical conditions, the teenager's doctor, the medical facility he or she prefers to use, and sometimes even a notary's signature and seal.

▲ If a teenager is injured, most medical facilities will want to make a copy of his or her medical/liability release form ***before*** proceeding with treatment.

Preparing a First Aid Kit

Any time you conduct a service project, make sure your group has a well-stocked first aid kit. If you don't have the resources to create a lengthy one like this, at least bring some of the basic items described here. This list should not be considered exhaustive as these are only some of the basic supplies one might need in the event of a minor accident.

Talk to a medical professional for advice on what to add to this list. Some denominational offices recommend specific types of first aid kits to their mission trip participants. In addition, read a first aid manual to discover other items to add to the list.

Adhesive bandages, assorted (box)	Ammonia capsules
Ace™ bandages (roll)	Instant cold pack
Triangular bandages (box)	Ointment for insect bites
Gauze, compress (pads)	Lotion for treating poison ivy, poison oak, rash
Gauze, compress (roll)	Acetaminophen or ibuprofen tablets
Butterfly bandages	Antacid tablets
Cotton balls or cotton swabs	Hydrocortisone cream
Tweezers	Facial tissue
Scissors	Resealable sandwich bags
Disposable waterproof gloves	Small paper bag
Thermometer	Small paper cups
Small mirror	Safety pins
Bandage tape (roll)	Hard candy or other source of sugar (for treating
Antibiotic cream	diabetic low blood sugar)
Sealed antiseptic/germicidal wipes	Small flashlight
Eye wash and eye-wash cup	First aid manual